Haunted Hills
& Hanging Valleys

Haunted Hills
& Hanging Valleys

Selected Poems 1969–2004

Peter Trower

HARBOUR PUBLISHING

Published by
Harbour Publishing Co. Ltd.
P.O. Box 219, Madeira Park, BC V0N 2H0
www.harbourpublishing.com

BRITISH
COLUMBIA
ARTS COUNCIL
Supported by the Province of British Columbia

Cover photograph by Michael Wigle
Edited and designed by Silas White
Printed and bound in Canada

THE CANADA COUNCIL | LE CONSEIL DES ARTS
FOR THE ARTS | DU CANADA
SINCE 1957 | DEPUIS 1957

Harbour Publishing acknowledges financial support from the Government of Canada through the Book Publishing Industry Development Program and the Canada Council for the Arts; and from the Province of British Columbia through the British Columbia Arts Council and the Book Publisher's Tax Credit through the Ministry of Provincial Revenue.

National Library of Canada Cataloguing in Publication

Trower, Peter, 1930-
        Haunted hills and hanging valleys : selected poems
1969-2004 / Peter Trower.

ISBN 1-55017-311-1

        1. Pacific Coast (B.C.)--Poetry. I. Title.

PS8589.R694H38 2004   C811'.54   C2004-901069-7

Contents

Foreword
Don McKay

When it comes to poetry, all labels mislead, especially those that are partly true. The term "logger poet," usually attached to Peter Trower, is one of those lying labels that cling because they're handy, not because they're apt. Of course we are right to think of the logging life in its broadest sense—including the rhythms of the work, the weathers, the landscape rendered in close detail, the characters and the tales—forming, early on, the bulk of his content. But what we really encounter in a Trower poem, whether it's one of the love poems written in recent years or an elegy for some lost landscape or person, is an ardent lyric presence, a presence that seems part folk philosopher, part impassioned witness, part pure singer.

In fact the changes wrought by Trower's work on the traditional logging verse of the bunkhouse ballad are so sweeping that, were it not for the common setting, there would be little reason to lump them together. Besides introducing a flexible free-verse line and a deeper sense of poetic form, he helped to rescue the matter of logging from its own larger-than-life mythology. Like goldrush miners, cowboys and professional athletes, loggers have cultivated their own legend, partly (I suspect) to bring narrative shape and meaning to one of the world's toughest, most dangerous occupations. It is easier to endure such risks knowing you're part of a larger, mythically proportioned set of stories, a romance structure with its own esprit de corps.

But while Peter Trower renovated the logging poem, he did so by adding realistic focus, emotional complexity and a frequently self-ironic narrator, not by dismissing the older tradition or diminishing our sense of true heroism of that hardscrabble existence. Trower relishes the tales and characters, but he sets them in a wider context and never lets their shapeliness and punch shoulder aside the "day to day blues" or the routine terrors of living with the rogue physics of steel cable slinging timber. It is tempting to sum this up by saying that he turns a tall tale into a wide one.

But perhaps it would be more accurate to compare it to the difference Conrad observes, in *Heart of Darkness*, between the tales of ordinary seamen and those of his narrator, Marlow.

> The yarns of seamen have a direct simplicity, the whole meaning of which lies within the shell of a cracked nut. But Marlow was not typical (if his propensity to spin yarns be excepted), and to him the meaning of an episode was not inside like a kernel but outside, enveloping the tale which brought it out only as a glow brings out a haze, in the likeness of one of these misty halos that sometimes are made visible by the spectral illumination of moonshine.

The tall tale or bunkhouse ballad celebrates a whole way of life with one broad brush; the Trower poem, like the Marlow fable, widens to include the surrounding landscape, the troubling aftermath, the constant peril and notably, in its emotional range, the elegy.

With this new selection, we have plenty of opportunity to observe how the "wide tale" works as a strategy for many other subjects, how appropriate it would be for us now to apply, provisionally, other epithets—love poet, nature poet, elegist—and so bring about a more just sense of Peter Trower's range and accomplishment. He is very much a nature poet in such poems as "Goliath Country," with its tight rhyming stanzas grieving the falling of giant timber.

> Birds circle bewildered
> in a scathing grey rain
> above this field of the fallen
> these huge slain.
> Cawing puzzlement
> they sideslip and swoop.
> The downed giants lie silent
> in more than sleep.

Or we could consider the pointed shift in perspective performed by "The Animals," away from the "mackinawed transgressors/ in mudcaked boots" to the marten ("a streamlined package of brown wariness"), deer and whisky-jacks. And a poem like "The Alders" is a useful reminder of the widening of the tale beyond the logger's perspective, since alders are the "reoccupiers" who fill in the "brown wounds" and bush roads after the loggers have moved on. Perhaps, in poems like these, "post-logger poet" would make a better label, if we had to have one. In other places we find that the poet's ample embrace of life focuses on one person, as in love poems like "A Wild Girl to Walk the Weathers With," and the many homages to specific characters like Annie of the Corridors, the popcorn man, or Louis Miranda, the "Language Keeper" who transcribed his native Squamish while living the life of a longshoreman.

One of these homages, "The King of Rhymes and Whistles," may have a special significance for Trower's own poetic voice, since its subject is the bunkhouse balladeer Robert Swanson, someone for whom that logger-poet label is pretty well an exact fit. Swanson's model was Robert Service, who had popularized the myth of the Klondike. Although they haven't achieved the fame accorded Dan McGrew and company, Robert Swanson's bunkhouse ballads were popular in logging camps up and down the coast and are arguably as tightly crafted and witty as those of the Yukon bard. An engineer and inventor (the "whistles" of Trower's title refers to a special air horn he invented for diesel trains), Swanson was able to tell rollicking rhymed yarns with one foot (okay, toe) in the realm of fact. So when Peter Trower came to write his homage, it was important not only to acknowledge Swanson's influence ("your ballads banged through my boyhood") and success (though Trower was writing poems, "the loggers had yours by heart, Bob Swanson"), but also to point to matters on which those bunkhouse ballads were silent, and which the young Trower found to be in good supply: "bugs, hellish weather and wall-to-wall danger." It is also interesting to note that, although Trower is here using a rough-hewn blank verse, it is possible to hear, like the clock ticking inside the crocodile in *Peter Pan*, the ghost of the old strongly stressed Swanson metre.

> Now you've hired out to those Holy Ghost camps
> with a rucksack of myths, a suitcase of echoes

leaving a boy in an aging man's body
still hearing your whistles and heeding your rhymes.

Working under the surface here is the stretch inside Trower's voice, the way he reaches back to include within his own craft that echo of the bunkhouse ballad.

Craft, it might be said, is the place where work and art meet, where they argue, barter and strike some sort of a deal. If we've read much poetry, we're probably familiar with the kind of deal we find in a lot of modernist writing, in which art "purifies the dialect of the tribe," lifting it out of the workplace into its own rarefied air. But strong work poets like Peter Trower exercise a pull in the other direction, reminding the angels of poesy of the workaday world that the tribe inhabits. Often he uses a comfortable free-verse line that has the ample reach and pace of Al Purdy, capable of carrying a poetic voice with close links to live speech. For brief stretches he will indulge in a lavish interlinear soundplay, letting the urge to song swell inside in a manner reminiscent of Dylan Thomas: after a bender the narrator gets home to "bed down blind in my clothes like an overdue corpse"; ravens "circle strange in the curdled sky"; the love of his life, Yvonne, is "a wild girl to walk the weathers with."

There is always an open, cheerful brawn to this bricolage, full of gestures that enjoy their own physical sway and chunk. A person thumbing through a glossary of logging terms—something Peter Trower has occasionally appended to his books—might well observe that, since it is already three-fifths of the way to poetry, loggers' argot is ready-made material for a poet. Donkeypuncher, hooktender, whistlepunk, chokerman, guthammer, truckjammer—it's an arsenal of consonant-clashing compounds, often dramatizing the fusion of man and machine in a compact nugget. It's clear Trower loves this lingo and extends its spirit into compounds of his own (stumpslopes, alleyscrapper, reamedout, endofnowhere), sometimes fashioning mini-poems like the *kenningar* of old Germanic prosody, metaphors that replace stock nouns with evocative images. In Old English we find "whale road" and "storm of swords" for ocean and battle; in Trower we find "woodwar" for logging, "forefathered ground" for graveyard, and "November's feathers" (which "twitch in the colourwrung sky") for snow. One whole poem is devoted to a celebration of fellow logger Barney Cotter's moment of poetic inspiration, when he applies the term "goosequill snags" to some old burnt-out cedars, "his only poetry." Throughout you can feel the force and fibre of the working life giving the craft its torque, enabling language to pick up its load with momentum and swing.

Instead of trying out provisional and inadequate labels, perhaps we should simply accept an epithet proposed by the poet himself. In one of his most sweetly lyrical poems, "Upwind from Yesterday," Trower calls himself a "bemused atavist" as he surveys the softening, forgiving effects of time on memory.

> Upwind from yesterday
> the shape of things alters and twists,
> the hurts diminish,
> the misapprehensions pack their bags.
> We are left with the trembling gist.

In fact many of the poems belong to a genre we might call the on-site elegy. Typically the narrator revisits some place rife with memories—ghost camp, cut-over hillside, failing pulp town, ruins of an old pub falling to the forces of gentrification—and reflects on the losses, an old soldier returning to a battlefield, paying tribute to bygone days without wishing them back. In a number of poems the bemused atavist reaches back to the pioneer days of BC logging to celebrate the pre-industrial loggers—the handfallers who could take two days felling a giant cedar with crosscut saws, or the bullpunchers who, before the arrival of the donkey engines and logging railroads, hauled logs with oxen. Notable among the on-site elegies is "The Last Spar-Tree on Elphinstone Mountain," a poem dedicated, appropriately, to Al Purdy. Alone on the ridge above the "battered mountain's back," the spar-tree that was once the hub and axis of an old "show" now evokes a complex of memories—high times and great perils—as well as the ethical dilemma of modern forestry.

It's either a cornfield or a catastrophe.
Either a crop or a tithe or a privacy
has been taken from this place.
What matter? It's done. Beyond that ridge is a valley
I helped hack and alter.

Without coming down on either side of the forestry propaganda war, the poet adds their claims to the other contending elements in the poem, the broken cables and rotten hemlock snags that clash with the great yarns, the "hillhumour" and even the "excellent shits behind stumps with the wind fanning the stink away." The poem ends, not with any resolution, but with a proposal that brings all those forces together in one potent and paradoxical symbol.

Dream on in peace, old tree—
perhaps you're a truer monument to man
than any rocktop crucifix in Rio de Janeiro.

And perhaps the abandoned spar-tree might also stand as a fitting emblem for the range and power of Peter Trower's poetry: the tree which is a tool which is a relic, testifying to the valour required by this rugged work, to the vanishing way of life it engendered, to the intense love-hate embrace of man and machine, and, of course, to the depth of our capacity, caught up in the machinery of capitalism, for destruction.

for Yvonne

As Long As the Wheel Turns Us

Meticulous bees stitch honeytrails
through the raspberries;
cat dreams camouflaged
in the Scotch broom's yellow shadow;
carpenters woodpecker walls
two tapping houses away.

Summer grey as a fogged glass
full of gull complaints;
distant heartbeat of boats
setting the metre of morning;
clouds have clapped their hands
over the mouth of the sun.

Last summer's ghost
hides around the house corner
holding a piebald cat
I gave to the garden earth.
Friends I drank to the days with,
girls who have slipped their moorings.

We're all another year
closer to our comeuppances—
the carpenters   the cat   the gulls
the bees   the ghosts   and me—
riding with time through the carousel seasons
as long as the wheel turns us.

On the Alexandra Bridge

Rendered obsolete
by cleverer technology
the castaway span still stands
joining two fragments of disused road
once a sterling accomplishment
now a rusting anachronism
like something after a nuclear war
when civilization has crumbled.

Graduation Day graffiti
disfigures the approaches
like all the rainbow rocks and cliffs
they've sullied with spray cans
but the bridge stands stolidly
leading from nowhere to nowhere
spanning a historic river
become history in turn.

Across that torrent now
is only a Native fish trap
the shore reverts to primal purposes.
You pick wild strawberries
by a wild orchard of cherry trees
I kiss your strawberry lips
and hold you close
at the dead span's centre
while the muddy flood churns beneath us
and Simon Fraser's ghost
laughs silently from the cliffs.

Goliath Country

Birds circle bewildered
in a scathing grey rain
above this field of the fallen
these huge slain.
Cawing puzzlement
they sideslip and swoop.
The downed giants lie silent
in more than sleep.

There has been great havoc here,
an enormous slaughtering.
Some David has run amok
with a relentless sling
leaving a broken green chaos
an apocalypse of wood
and a new void in the universe
where Goliaths once stood.

They will come to remove the bodies
while the echoes still linger
in driven chariots, driven
by the hard ancient hunger.
Birds circle bewildered
like men long travelled
who return to find their homes gone
and the town levelled.

Atlantic Crossing

Shipping from Liverpool on a gunpowder morning
cloudy weeks before the Blitz
from a city under barrage-balloons
in Dunkirk-shocked June
the year the madman howled for power,
John Bull stepped cigar-faced from his picture
and somewhere beyond the frightened island
Europe was cutting her throat again.

Slipping from Liverpool past a crippled cruiser
a shell-hole through her bowplates
crying the numb truth of war
in a strangled steel voice,
the year the wheels of the world turned
sixteen notches to the bad
and there was a bitter smell in the air
of something elemental and perverse.

But not for us, the fool children
of that belief-strained time
chasing through the loud bowels of the ship
our nine-year-old tails
dancing in the mercy of our ignorance
through the oblivious charades of childhood
while adults with dire tense faces
whispered nervous knowledge along the aisles.

For there were things more sinister than sharks
nosing bluntly through the dark,
searching through the smoked-glass gulfs
for the elusive engine rhythms,
swimming with a bellyful of bombfish
toward the betraying metal heartbeats
bound for sternweather latitudes
where Titanics call from black fathoms.

But we followed the marigold girls
of our first uncomplicated urges
at second-class gift counters
bought them worshipful toy pandas
while the universe was caving in
like a drunk man in a bar
the countries of common sense collapsing
into deathcamps and cinders.

On the afterdeck, a clear-voiced blind boy
sang sad songs of hope and parting,
waiters sought to entertain us
by pretending to pull off their thumbs,
spectral iceberg islands
haunted the path that arced to Greenland,
the grey hunters fell behind us,
the remote land reduced itself to dreams.

They shut off the engines for precaution.
We drifted silent for two days
in the fog somewhere east of Labrador
like a great dead whale in the dark.
We, the fool children, still laughed
lacking the comprehension for true terror
but the first-class millionaires shuddered,
the stewards went white about their work.

It was the ill-fated ship's last run.
Her luck spilled out of her like sand
when she moved toward England again
through those deadly waters.
A torpedo took her amidships—
she went down like a gutshot duck—
into the kitchens of the uttermost deep
went all the brave and friendly waiters.

The Railway Ghosts

They stumble up the stairs sometimes
the frayed time-scuttled men
in rumpled suits, searching
for long-mislaid friends
at vanished pool and poker tables—
perhaps a random lady love
wistfully remembered
from nights of rum and laughter
when Mae West McKersky
sang them whiskey tunes
and smoky railroad stories
rattled across the room.

They stand displaced, uncertain,
bewildered in the glitz and change—
never-before-seen faces,
expressing vague curiosity, or nothing,
float about them along the altered bar,
above the transformed tables,
whispering no particular welcome.
Someone has pulled the plug on yesterday.

They fumble up the stairs sometimes
the frayed time-scuttled men
but Mae West McKersky
has long since sold the premises
and only sings in dreams now.
The past has highballed away
like a runaway freight on a bad grade
leaving only what future there is
shadow-tracking out ahead.

The frayed time-scuttled men
turn on worn heels
descend the going-nowhere-now stairs
move slowly back into what is and must be
tomorrow shunting them beyond
this tipsy whistle-stop
that is theirs no longer.

Grandaddy Tough

Grandaddy Tough's
got a history of logging
in his muscles.
The cold-decked memories
lie eager for the telling.

He's old and young—
the manfires
smoulder yet in him.
He has stripped more sidehills
than I'll ever know.
Lost spar-trees
shudder in his eyes.

He has walked with legends
and all unknowing
become one,
beyond the heyday of his boots
the forests thrown down
regrown
and thrown down again.

He roars yet
in the power of his age,
a leather veteran
of the mountain wars
splendid in drink,
a thousand bar chairs behind him
since the first lifted whiskey,
the first fat stake
pissed grinning down the drain.

In the sweaty dusk
of forgotten bunkhouses
he has gambled with dead rigging rats
and tumbled to his bunk
to sleep the timber sleep.

Among boys he walks
careless with experience.
Grandaddy Tough,
a bridge of gristle
between then and now.

The steampots, the skylines
rust on crippled ridges
but he lurches on
under trees of steel
in the knotty triumph of his trade.

Machinery in the Mountains

Once a madman told me
there was machinery in the mountains
a hidden complex of cogs and wheels
turning eternally under the world.
"Mark my words," he babbled
"the hills will open one day
like the backs of watches
in a judgment of wonder
baring the teeth and the truth of it.
You will see."

There was a cockeyed logic
to his lunacy
in guileless boyhood
I almost believed him
till the years eroded my innocence
and his crazed talk drummed into memory.

But every so often, the fancy returns
that myth of millennial clockwork
clicking forever behind the façade.
Sometimes I stand on mountains
and I swear I can hear those ghostly wheels
turning faint as a whisper
grinding away like the engines of God
in the secret guts of the peaks.

Grease for the Wheels of Winter

Quickening in the valley, the white flutter
blurs the road-slashed relief map   the valley floor
tips in the salted distance   such damp confetti
will wed these boondocks to quiet.

But yet, the engines grunt   lines tighten and thrash
against the spooked sky   men stamp and laugh
beside hemlock fires   trucks wheeze   remote radio voices
direct woodwar   we are still at our bothersome business.

And then we are shrugging from skins of wet raingear
lighting cigarettes   eating apples   lying a mean lick
rattling toward warmth in the quitting-time crummy
past killed machines like abandoned yellow elephants.

Behind us, the old house of the land reclaims silence.
Soon the snow will cover the broken floors and furniture
        with a single sheet.
No one will unlock these doors again until spring.
Rigging will hang like forgotten laundry
        from clothesline-pole spar-trees.

Only the wind will come then to croon in the spared boughs
of trees too high or meagre to kill   the white, the white
flutter and smile of silence will spread from ear to ear
and nod this place calm like a mother.

A Testament of Hills

It was pulling strawline
up some endofnowhere hill
in the rain
with the whole world tied to the end—
reefing like a lunatic
on a piece of steel string
with no hand free to swat the horseflies.

It was Friday afternoons
of drythroats and beerthirst,
wahooing down washouts
with the quitting-time whistle
sounding reprieve—
shave and a haircut
six bits.

It was riding those doodlebug planes
up craggy inlets—
bouncing through the airpockets
in gutgrabbing skips and hops
to land with queasy relief,
caulk boots and a duffle bag
at some forlornshack camp.

It was a block breaking
with a spar-tree half raised—
the tree smashing back into the swamp—
part of the block whistling by your head
like angry shrapnel
and in your mouth, the rusty taste of death
for the first time.

It was trying to unhook floating logs
with greenhorn fingers
in the churning bullpen
of an A-frame show—
the hardnosed engineer
busting a gut with laughter
each time you hit the shivering drink.

It was sometimes the inviting eyes
of a faller's wife
dangerous with discontent and townhunger,
bored with isolation and her husband's
rough and seldom hands,
enticing reluctant chokerboys
into scared-stiff affairs.

It was the cool-eyed logger junkies
kicking heroin habits in sullen bunkhouses,
cynical victims of too many
underworld winters,
boasting of successful scores,
getting back in shape for another
tussle with the monkey.

It was the wattled faces
of reamedout oldtimers
reduced to bedmaking
and shrill recollection,
watching the crummies and campboats leave
for the steep morning hills
in arthritic envy.

And it was deadly dull
bunkshack Sundays
in the windy lonesome wilderness
relieved by the toothless wit
of the camp comic
who knew every dirty joke there was
and a few more.

It was working three suicide shows
in a row
too broke or stupid to quit—
logs and boulders crashing down on you
through blinding clammy fog—
an uprooted stump chasing you one day
and nearly catching you.

It was the skidroad hiring halls
with their seedy wheedling mancatchers—
their beckoning job-listing blackboards
and the travel vouchers that committed you
to early-morning airstrips
and another resigned plunge
into the familiar unknown.

It was letting the last guyline go
on a stripped spar-tree—
watching it quiver and topple
like a sabotaged tower
to crash back to earth
in a second downfall
for only raised trees died more than once.

It was the legendary characters—
Dirty Dick,
Boomstick Annie,
Eight-and-Biscuits Bronson,
Johnny on the Spot—
some actually met in careless camps,
most remaining myths.

It was walking to the wharf
on listless Jervis Inlet evenings
full of impatient energy
even the sidehills couldn't sap—
yearning for the bright lights
and that elusive something beyond them
you couldn't quite name.

And it was unreal early shifts
in the tinder days of fireseason
standing on dim slopes
as light crawled over the farthest ridge,
beating off the insects
who ruled the summer dawns,
hearing the starting whistle blow.

It was fighting fire—
wearing backpacks and eating smoke,
tugging hoses through a no man's land
of sparks and charcoal,
sitting all-night watch
with the mountain smouldering around you
like a medieval hell-vision.

It was evil days of high wind and hail
with saplings snapping like straws
and your hands numb
and your mind numb
and your feet soaking wet
and a log-hungry company-loving hooker
too chintzy to shut her down and go home.

It was the ubiquitous cookshack
centre of every camp's humdrum universe
where the grub was sometimes good,
sometimes bad, but always plentiful
and once you saw a cook take after a man
with a meat-cleaver
just like in Bob Swanson's poem.

It was the beer-parlour bull sessions
where the toughest shows were yarded,
the highest log-counts taken,
the tallest trees topped,
the closest shaves experienced
and every whistlepunk
was hooktender for a night.

It was three glum months
on an obscure stinking tideflat
somewhere northeast of nowhere
where the rain was constant,
wolves prowled at night
and once the boatman got drunk with the supplies
and you went on short rations for a week.

And it was the last camp,
the deadliest show of them all,
ground so treacherous
the hooktender whistled in disbelief.
You stuck it out for awhile
but the fear got you in the end
so you quit the logging camps forever—
until the next time.

The Alders

The alders are the reoccupiers
they come easily
and quick into skinned land
rising like an ambush on raked ridges
jabbing like whiskers
up through the washed-out
faces of neverused roads.

The alders are the forestfixers
bandaging brown wounds
with applegreen sashes
filling in for the fallen firs
jostling up by the stumps
of grandfather cedars
leaning slim to the wind
by logjammed loggerleft streams.

The alders are the encroachers
seizing ground the greater trees owned
once
but no more.

It is the time of the alders.
Like a bright upstart army
they crowd the deadwood spaces
reaching
at last for the hand of the whole
unshadowed sun.

Appointed Rounds

It was some goddamn cold that December!
Even my thoughts almost froze sometimes
as I trudged with my sack of Christmas homilies
bills   benisons   scribbled babble
a bag full of nothing and everything
to pop through slots like paper coins
activating ghosts in half the haunted houses
along my route   twenty-five grudging bucks a week
was all those pennypinchers paid that tight winter.
In return for their parsimony
we dumped all the junkmail off bridges
into gullies and canyons
watched those unwanted ads and circulars
flutter down the wind to fitting oblivion.
It was like unloading ballast
always half expecting some livid postal inspector
to leap from behind a lamppost
threatening dire consequences.
What a fine illegal feeling when none came!
My heart lightened like my burden
I moved more willingly now along snow-bearded sidewalks
to aloof orange-haired nurses in private sanitariums
silent starched nuns in shadowy convents
alcoholic old maids in lavender living rooms
who sometimes offered me drinks
affluent Chinese wives in immaculate bungalows
burned-out trainmen who always wanted to talk
once an English teacher from years back
who thought I would have become a writer by now—
I muttered excuses feeling I'd failed him miserably.
Always I stopped at the same trusting drugstore
to slip furtive pocketbooks into my near-empty sack
for who'd suspect a true-blue mailman anyhow
even such a part-time tyro as I was?

At last the last house and letter
back to the district depot of squinting sorters
hunched on their Cratchit stools
punchy from names and addresses
to drop off the bag   mission completed, mister
for another grey day. Soon busbound home
thoughts thawing   five dollars richer.
Man, it was sure some goddamn cold that December!

The Millionglitter

They have prospered and grown strong
in deep drumming fathoms
learned what the tides sing
in the long secret deeps
now their common time has come
the silver swarms gather
their biding years are over
there is an old tryst to keep.

The fish   the men
close on their collision course
the mercury armadas
flicker to the call
round instinctive eyes
programmed only for rivers
guileless of webbed ambush
the waiters at their wheels.

The men sit like patient spiders
on their waterspun webs
last year was a lean one
they hope this will be better
it's all up to the fish
who move because they must
toward the staked-out coast
in a millionglitter.

The Ridge Trees

Distantly on stone ridges
the highest trees lean wearily
like old men
in Japanese paintings
shuffling eternally before the wind.

Helicopter clacks down the valley
chopper preceding the choppers
airborne timber tallier
counting the moneyherds
of the untouched conifers.

Next year we will practise havoc
in that green trench—
the saws will yammer their nagging dirge,
the donkeys will gather the corpses,
the land will be hammered to stumps and ruin.

And when our depredations are done
only the twisted ridge trees will stand
above the brown carnage
like meditative old men
shuffling eternally before the wind.

The Last Handfallers

They're coming up the trail
big blue-veined hands
cramped from a lifetime
of tyrannical wooden handles
of gnawing the big ones down
the hard way
of hearing the undercut timber cry
as it grudgingly gives.

They have stoical Svenska faces
white-stubbled
cured to creased red leather
by a many-weathered craft.

They have crinkled Svenska voices
like wind in the branches
of the countless killed trees
who have given them their tongues.

They are older than rumours
unbending as mountain granite.
They have been lured from boozy retirement
to fall the West Fork setting.

With their tedious crosscuts
they will topple the rockslide cedars
spitting snoose
hoping to lessen the breakage.

They have returned to the resinous hills
like ancestral gunslingers
for one final showdown
with the reluctant trees.

The Finishing

Last day   last hour   last log
big grizzled fir butt
lead-heavy with pitch   seesawing
on the lip of a hundred-foot hole.
There's two or three more good pieces
down in that spooky pit.
They can bloody well stay there—
only a chopper could harvest those bastards.

Last day   last hour   last log
I take my time with it   easing
ragged cable around rough bark
in the familiar ritual.
I punch the whistle   the choker snaps taut
the fir butt shakes alive,
shudders up from its deathbed,
crunches toward the spar-tree.

Last day   last hour   last log
a sense of relief   a sense of sadness.
Now I will run in the lines and blocks—
we have had our way with this mountain,
another woodwar won,
another forest felled and stolen,
another notch on some timber king's desk—
another virgin hill ahead of us.

Bullpuncher

In the old man's spiderscrawl you read:
"My grandaddy was a teamster.
Worked the woods for Jerry Rogers
back round 1862."
Something tugs from a long distance:
new trees slide back into the ground,
old trees rise like lost sentries
and you are more him than you
in the rumbling belly of the past
tasting whiskey, wanting more. And women!
Stamping through Gassy Jack's on Saturday
with last week's wages in your hand—
sure like to bed that pretty young one
but you ain't handsome and you smell bad.
Fat Bessie with the bad teeth
is all you're ever bound to find.
The madam with her hand out,
whorehouse piano tinkling bright brassy ditties,
brief tumbles on soiled backroom sheets—
then it's back to the bullteams, the hollering,
checking harnesses and chainhooks,
bound to get a few more weeks' hauling
before the deep snow.

Bound to shout 'em uptrail   downtrail
till the light won't allow it—
sends you trudging down the skidroad home
for more bacon and navy beans,
maybe fresh biscuits if you're lucky
and that bellyrobber didn't burn 'em,
certainly coffee strong as gall
and later on, the old complaints
that men have always made in bunkhouses
in army barracks   in mine cages—
in ship's holds   assuredly in jail
when the warders couldn't hear
till the lamps are snuffed at 9:30.
You drop like a hog into a hole
too spent to dream more than simply
of anything except trees and damp,
drown into oblivion like a sea
till it's daylight in the swamp
the bulls wait patient for your goadstick,
someone curses groggily   your socks stink,
outside it's still raining
you grunt numbly through the motions
the guthammer writes strident on the air
the cold truths of morning.

The Animals

The second marten
I've ever seen
eyes us in glittering assessment
before moving rapidly along a dead log
a streamlined package of brown wariness
to become the forest again.

Two deer
deploy through the distance
tiptoe nervously
through the first thin snow
watch curiously
as we fumble cold cables.

Only the whisky-jacks
display any regret
vying for our lunchtime leavings
with an extra grey urgency
to top off winter caches
in obscure hollow trees.

November's feathers
twitch from a colourwrung sky
settling like a white moss of reprieve
on the wrecked hill.
Blood oozes from a hemlock stump
as I savage its bark with a powersaw.

We are mackinawed transgressors
in mudcaked boots
cursing and blessing the freighted wind
as the day dwindles
the season takes aim on us
and the animals know.

Kisses in the Whiskey

When the kisses were still in the whiskey
and Sally Singer peddled her hips
along Granville Street in winter neon
for trick money and occasional tips,
we moved in up-collared topcoats
daggery black shoes flashing bright
past Sammy the spastic newsboy
like bogus gangsters in the night.

With our tender boy-faces shamming tough,
cigarettes nailed to them,
the truths of life staggered obviously by
but we looked through them.
In our tight-cuffed alleyscrapper pants
we threaded through the late-night bustlers,
middleclass kids in hoodlum drag
trying to fake that we were hustlers.

But we never thought of it that way—
we were happy at our Friday games
with our mickey bottles in our pockets
eyeing all the easy dames.
We were transfixed by all those flashy chicks
although we seldom caught any.
Sweet Sally Singer would have fixed us up
but we never had her kind of money.

I wish I could be that ignorant again
embarked on some sophomoric fling
far too callow to understand
that life is other than a Friday thing.
I miss our vanished naive selves
young as spring colts and just as frisky
when Sally Singer peddled her hips
and there were still kisses in the whiskey.

Unmarked Doorways

The booze cans of yesteryear
lurk along Granville Street
unmarked doorways like blind eyes
between the bookie joints
and dirty book stores
with buzzers and "Joe sent me" peepholes
latterday speakeasies
of the deadbeat Sixties
filled with rounders   roustabouts
rummies   racetrackers   reprobates
and wry rouged women who've seen better days
slumped on couches and kitchen chairs
knocking back bad whiskey and tap water
from grubby plastic glasses
four-bits a shot
while Satchmo and Lady Day
sing "My Sweet Hunk of Trash"
on the wonky phonograph.

Old illicit nights on the lowlife drag
after the pubs have packed up
and only the diehards are left
bleary-eyed in the graveyard hours
thinking what they might have been
before the city swallowed them
dreams and all
sucked them down whole
into its underbelly
to huddle behind the anonymous doors
of the blind pigs
sharing their common loneliness
with bootleggers and bandits
like refugees
from some obscure war
a legion of losers
in the neon-winking dark
bottlemates   boon companions
of the beleaguered years.

The Popcorn Man

All summer sad he stood
by English Bay with a glass barrow
counting his slow regrets.
Heat crept and slid in the greasy streets;
he grew there quiet as a tree.
Children buzzed him like gnats.

If he'd had a barrel organ, a monkey,
he might have made music
instead of hollow buttered fluff
but he made no music—few words—
a handful of dime-at-a-time dollars.
The stray dogs nipped at his cuffs.

A tall brown ghost of a man
blurred somehow like a faded photograph
he haunted the boardwalk.
At night or in rainy weather
he haunted the room across the hall.
Once we talked.

The loneliness broke free from him like moths
the solemn voice scratched painful memory
from griefdusty grooves:
the war wound   the stolen wife   the coal mines
the heart attacks   the doctor's stern edict.
His words fell down the air like dead leaves.

Three wasted winelost days later
I returned from sodden odysseys.
His door was ajar—
it was out of keeping with his habits
(he was private as a spider)—
I dared my head round the door.

He lay naked facing the wallpaper
at least two days reprieved from agony
half his body blue as the sky
as razor blades
as the sea he never swam in or sailed
only watched sometimes with remote yearning eyes.

They buried him in Potter's Field
I stayed on in that musty roominghouse—
there was no need to be afraid.
Not of Jake, the lost popcorn man—
he'd had a bellyful of haunting.
He took his ghost with him when he died.

Sailor

for Grant Cattanach

In the sinister season
the mountains pull down the rain
endless threads and wet filaments
anchor the earth to the battleship clouds
blockade the sun
paint the world the colour of nothing
hold November over our heads
like a threat.

I am reading an eight-year-old letter
in the grip of this gaunt month.
You were safe in your odysseys then
the words sprawl joyously
spill coast to coast across the continent
linger on girls quickmet in Montreal
trigger that long-lost pen
in the bunk of a freighter throbbing to Amsterdam.

Voice from the wanderlust years
discontented with mills and camps
you shipped with your own tides
laughed back from beyond with a seabag of insights
but the needles stitched your path crooked
the sailor joys ebbed away
the drugs drove you inward to weave
a curtain of pain you could not speak through.

A hunter came on you by chance
two miles deep in an untravelled valley.
Beneath a tree   past grief or reason
you had signed your final sailing papers.
You have left November like a country
bound for indistinct shores
leaving us here on the chill docks of fall
eating the words we never said.

Along Green Tunnels

Along green tunnels
sinewy alders thrust up from the salmonberries
growth foams across old roads like gates closing
grouse rustle secretly
slugs move like severed yellow fingers
shrinking mudpools remember the last rain
sunshafts stab through the leaves
and I walk in a troglodyte strangeness
knowing summer's begun.

Beyond these living caves
the eternal clouds have shredded
the coconut world gleams
it is as it should be—
after battering weeks of rain
the leaves suck light
above these emerald passageways
dream its sugar down to their roots,
perform their purpose.

In the green tunnels
there is a universe of reaffirmation
I walk through witched green twilight
in suspicions of truth.
Rain comes, rain goes. In these aisles
in this trenched incredible quiet
I am one below summer
burning in the neutral wood.

Where Roads Lead

Empty signboard nailed to a tree
like a face without features
gives me no directions   I
need none anyway   the day
draws me with warm hands
up this rough and vacant road
to rocky vantage points where others
have paused to gaze on stillwood gullies
watertanks and houses torn
from wilderness   no wind   the small
far hill I'd love to build
a castle on   the vein-blue mountains
between   beyond, the sunflecked
spectrum of the sea.

Turn to the brush   the lure
of the land urges me on
up branch roads leading
past abandoned homesteads
where only weeds keep watch now
to stand in the gutted shell of a house
that has lost its people
and sinks into the green tide of the bushes
with cobwebbed windows
and still a rusty lock on the door
where some hesitant hand
turned the key on yesterday.

Today, I seek where roads lead
into my mind and out as I move them through me
and move along them, and move
through the questioning day.

But I know in my heart they are circular
twisting back on themselves like Mobius strips
like tail-devouring snakes
in this roundabout riddle
there are no real destinations.

Running the Euclataws

Past Shoal Bay
where a mining metropolis
was once laid out and abandoned
we abandon ourselves to the rapids—
white wargames
of water against water
yaw us this way and that—
the first whirlpool
wheels enormous
off our left bow.

We dodge each vortex nimbly
like nervous soldiers picking
their way through minefields,
the contesting tides
knot and froth.
I think of logs sucked down from booms
of boats turned turtle, men overboard
spun down till their eardrums burst—
this narrow throat has swallowed
much in its time.

We run the gauntlet of currents
and suddenly, unable to veer
strike one churning funnel head-on—
the boat slams sideways
like a shot dog before
the full brute strength of the Euclataws.
We taste their maelstrom kiss.

Upright again
a shade less nonchalant
we shake through the weakening fringes
to Stuart Island
with its autographed cliffs
where bored, impatient, outbound fishboats
await the bulltide's pleasure.

The Corkscrew Trees of Kitselas

The corkscrew trees of Kitselas
twist up from the primeval moss
of the ancient forest
as though two giant hands
had wrung them like dishrags.

Strange trees
coiling like brown narwhal horns
toward the thin October sun—
anomalies of nature
among their arrow-straight cousins.

Yet fitting symbols somehow
for this curious country
where black bears wear white coats
ancient lava flows wear blankets of green lichen
and the old hills wear history like a ceremonial robe.

The Reclaimed

Overwhelmed homesteads
lie crushed to the dirt
by adamant snows,
their waterlogged boards
mummybrown huddles
engendering moss,
arrogant blackberries
scratch through their ribs.

Tottering fenceposts
like battledrunk troops
groggy with rot
adavance into nowhere—
stagnating sockets,
bucketless wells
breed in their dimness
an airforce of gnats.

Sometimes a chimney
revealed like a trick
rears redbricked
from a scrimshaw of creepers.
Winds of conjecture
retrace a room
on the unhindered air,
the echoes of fire.

Stricken to phantoms
the feeders of dreams—
lost among stars
the sparks of their laughter.
All the wide hopes
the gadfly illusions
whimper from bedsprings
and rustgutted stoves.

Wordless the epitaph
decades have wrought—
vanishing paths
weedthrottled, forgotten;
impotent schemes
abandoned endeavours—
quick in her seasons
the earth will reclaim them.

Industrial Poem

That night, Slim Abernathy
pushed the wrong button and wrapped his best friend
three times around a driveshaft
in directions bones won't bend.

They shut her down and eased him out
broken most ways a man can break
yet he clung to his ruin for twenty-four hours
like a man to a liferaft for his death's sake.

They'd hardly hurried him away from there
as we stood around shockdrunk, incapable of help
when they cranked those expensive wheels up again,
started rolling out more goddamn pulp.

"Hamburger for lunch tonight, boys!"
joked a foreman to the crew.
I wish he'd smelled our hate but he never even flinched
as the red-flecked sheets came through.

When the Mill Was Our Mother

It dreams on in green memory
that small shabby outport
jammed between woods and water
in a sun-forsaken place
where life proceeded slowly
to the mill's growling edicts,
where time was kept by shift whistles
below the hooded mountain's face.

When the mill was our mother
orchestrating the days—
an erratic-tempered mother
of timber, brick and rank smells.
An uncouth mother
of belching stacks and old machinery.
A strict-minded mother
bending us surely to her will.

Yet a nurturing mother
who deeded us a town to live in
tumbledown   without pretensions
on the rainy river's brink
full of tarpaper palaces
with pulp-lined interiors,
full of simple caring people,
full of truth and common strength.

Like one family we lived
in the lost times   the unforgotten times
in the lean times   the rough and ready times
that were not like any other.
In that kingdom of friendly destiny
we had nothing   we had everything
by the tossing seas of silver yesterday
when the mill was our mother.

Running Scared with the Sky-Hanger

Bill, you old sky-hanger,
rigging a tree once, so thumping drunk
you didn't remember doing it
monkeying that stick by sheer
subliminal savvy
roping, spiking stubbornly up
to stand at the top like a blasphemous muezzin
knocking free bark with a blunt axe
blistering the air with curses
calling God to account.

Bill, you sidehill spider,
the Compensation Board would have screamed
in outrage to watch the day
you rode the bull-block up the spar
for the mad sake of speed
and later as we gulped to see it
unfastening your climbing rope,
tightrope walking along the skyline
a hundred and twenty feet above the stumps
to oil the carriage.

No, it was not the giddy hazards you feared
but something much more nebulous—
an obscure nemesis chewing like rust
at the guywires of your sanity.

Once in a back room at a weekend party
you showed me your private arsenal—
twenty-five loaded guns in a secret trunk,
even a Smith and Wesson.

"No one fucks with me, kid!"
you declared unsurely,
sweating terror
like an enemy in your eyes,
knowing the brain's blackest hounds
need only one careful bullet.

Outhouse

Nothing left in sight
but that crazy sentrybox outhouse
a simple man's totem
standing guard
over oysters cobbling
greengrey rocks
starfish orange and purpling
the lost bay's bottom
wary seal backsliding
into the calm deeps quick with fish.

Brush has buried the rest.
Thirty years of wild growth erased
the garden in the gully.
The garbage heap tells how long—
bottles and cans from belly-up companies
gleam and rust in an alder thicket

Those fragile skull-eyed shacks
hard to find on a tanglewood ridge
are empty as a whore's smile—
no trace of who or why.
A few more snows and winds will flatten them,
groundrot chew their boards to mulch.

But not the outhouse—
it'll stand for awhile yet.
Built for the wars, that crapper
fashioned solid and lovingly
with even scrollwork around the eaves
straddled on two skookum logs
over the narrow creek mouth.
Self-flushing—
an ingenious joy of a john.

It must have been his favourite place
to sit with ruminative pipe
on bird-busy evenings
planning a confident kingdom
to last at least forever.

First Dance

With a twist of the wrist
I went out and got pissed
sings Slim Bankhead in nineteen forty-two
the world's burning into bombsmoke
beyond this backwater place
as he courts my friend Bob's older sister
in the pulpmill town
among the smells   witchdark Vera
who stirs more than she knows
in my twelve-year-old loins till I squirm
with unfamiliar jealousy hating cocky Slim
when he kisses her in corners   her earthy
Italian mother baking bread   humming   approving
pretending not to notice   *Good*
son-in-law material that one   her millweary father dozing
behind a western pulpmag in the pulplined
tarpaper shack   it's New Year's Eve
first dance I've ever gone to   Bob and me
watching the grown-ups spin exultantly
through tipsy waltzes and foxtrots
in the piano-tinkling hall with its ecstatic
streamers and balloons   bottles circulate
quick as rumours   emancipated
girls of the wartime mill doing men's jobs
making men's money and hay
while the rain shines   switching through the glitter
with the few exempted bachelors   Squeezebox Eddie
coaxing the oldies from his deft
accordion   married women flirting
in best dresses with the wrong husbands   kids
and housework forgotten   Gimpy Gus Hogan
limp somehow transcended dipping
the ladies through strangely graceful
three-quarter-time twirls   pear-shaped Shoulders Kirk
with his dislocated slouch and black serge suit
pumping his partners around the floor
like a small frenzied ape   all too soon, mad midnight

hoots   horns   kissing   never saw adults act
so crazily before except through forbidden
Saturday-night beer-parlour windows   suddenly
crimson-lipped Vera homing in
like a vision through the clutching crowd   bussing Bob and me
both soundly on the lips   *Oh God!*   I can smell
her perfume   feel, weak with dim joy, her black
hair brushing my face   now I know for certain I'm
going to marry her when I grow up no matter what
the hell with Slim Bankhead   headily
I can taste her lovely lipsticked mouth
for weeks.

Second Skeleton

Letter from a girl fallen
over the edge of herself
received on a pale day
when clouds have risen
like blister tissue
on the sunburned sky.

Letter from a girl finished
with unmanageable realities
for a time of no telling—
given to sedated wards
where they will endeavour to untie
the hurting knots of anger.

You have been with me in this garden
beside the cornmothers cradling
their ragdoll cobs. I have sensed
the pressure of your tension—
the twisted uglier part of you
beneath the pretty,
that symbiotic entity of dread and self-hate
who lives like a second skeleton
in all of us, thriving hungrily
on what we wish worst for ourselves,
battening on our frets and terrors.

When you were last here
only your anguish held you upright
as the thin stakes shakily support
the tomato plants.

I wanted somehow
to stroke your agonies calm,
to starve the entity of your hurt,
to soothe you with whatever love I know.

But I, too, carry a malignant passenger.
Though I often try to drown him silent
he steers my cowardice like a ship.

Letter from a girl gone searching
for help in a likelier direction.
May the pain assuagers grant you
a few good secrets of peace.

Not-So-Still Life with Damp Beer Tables

We were sitting with the madgirl
on New Year's Eve
or the day after
and there wasn't much
rhyme or reason to it.

She said:
"I got wrists
like anyone else, see?"
and she showed them to me.

There were five white worms
across one
and three
across the other.

She said:
"You're supposed to be a poet,
baby.
What do you think of those poems?"

I said:
"Those are the saddest poems
I've ever read,"
and watched my buddy, bleak boy,
screwing her with his eyes.

Booby Trap

As though two hands held it bending
the small alder curves tight
over the thin creek that goes dry in summer.
It is spring. We blunder about
pretending to be fallers
through eleven acres of boggy bottomland.

Powersaws grumbling,
our own grumbling,
the crash of that rotten right-of-way timber—
no matter which way we undercut them
they keep dropping crooked and counter.
No trusting those devious trashtrees.

Steady dribble of rain,
an argument by the thin creek.
I stand back twisting a smoke.
He touches the chain to the bowed tree—
the tension explodes:
it splits like a sprung trap.

Fourteen feet
that mule-kicking alder barberchairs back,
catches me clean in the crotch—
tears the fly right out of my jeans
flings me flat on my ass
vibrates above me dangerously humming.

"You okay?" he yells, running over
our minor dissension forgotten.
"Guess so," I mutter uncertainly
so close to a eunuch it doesn't bear dwelling on.
We are two green fools falling—
around us the woods hiss disappointment.

Graveyard Shift

I am walking through Alcan's inferno
with Luigi Milanas
expatriate ex-paratrooper
at 4:30 in the glum
potline morning
sucking scorched air
down aisles of popping flame
only our millwright coveralls
distinguishing us from the grubby goblins
in thick brown pants without pockets
who tend to their functions and fires
making aluminum   bad lungs   good money
by luciferian light.

The cranes crash past above us
carrying snouted crucibles
to suck the magma from the pits
like ants from a hill.
Men ride three-wheeled crustbreakers
to rattling battle, lashing airhose tails
they peck at the pot-edges like birds.
Greasy yellow lift-trucks
clatter through the ruckus
driven on sullen errands
by Germans who still mourn Hitler—
buzzers   sweat   salt tablets
goggles   face masks   the taste of smoke—
I dream of the roasting voltage
pumping like blood through transformers
into these alchemic halls
to powerdance through the cathodes
cooking the bauxite silver
the careless, black
and the careless black of Sally's hair
and Black Label beer. . .
I fall asleep on my feet
and walk into a wall.

It's our once-nightly tour of duty
After this, if all is well
we can doze in the orangepeel lunchrooms
drink robot soup and cocoa
thumb through dog-eared skinbooks
till punchout time. But not tonight because
a crane has broken down
at the south end of Line Number Two.

"Let's go," says Luigi, sadly.

Collision Course

It is a tree of average girth
neither the tallest nor the smallest
it has rolled with the punches
of a hundred mountain storms
and weathered every one.

He is the sort of fastidious faller
who mixes his gas with a measuring cup
his boots are carefully greased
they crunch through the remnant snow
he carries the powersaw casually like a suitcase.

The tree shudders
as the chain rips through its growth rings
the man guides his tool impassively
thinking about his wife and kids
chips spray like shrapnel
the engine growls like a wounded cougar
fibres part before blurring teeth
the tree quakes   begins to inch
unwillingly from the vertical.

The man withdraws the saw   snaps it silent
leans against a stump   gropes for a smoke
on a tearing hinge of wood
the tree tips   hisses down
but the faller's aim has been faulty
the hemlock strikes a standing cedar
the butt breaks free   kicks back
like a triggered piston.

There is no time to run
the butt connects like a wooden hoof
pins the man to the stump
his ribs snap like sticks
fastidious to the end
he pulls free his wallet
places it safely above the blood
on the tree that has felled him.

Goosequill Snags

Barney Cotter
bought it up in Ramsay Arm.
Read it in the papers
twelve years back.
Wild log rolling-pinned on him
crushed him against a rock.

Barney and I worked together
in Halsam's camp on Goatfoot Mountain
with his chattering chuckle
that broke to a graveyard cough
hurting his way ahead of me up the slopes
burned out from booze and board feet at forty-five.

Barney was philosophical:
"That's the name of the game," he'd say
squinting out from under his hard hat
firing another cigarette.
"Always wanted to run a store or something
But I ended up a goddamn logger!"

There were a lot of dead trees on that claim
hollow fire-gutted cedar shells
spiking up among the felled timber.
"Goosequill snags," Barney called them.
I never forgot the term—
it was his only poetry.

Barney is long buried
but his goosequill snags still stand
on the mending slopes of Goatfoot Mountain.
Lonely monuments
to another man the hills took
writing his rough legend on the sky.

Skookumchuck

Reprieved for a merciful moment
from repetitive conversation
in the ramshackle evening bunkhouse,
I watch the alders move like great grey reeds
to a wrinkling wind
below the ruined watersheds and wrung slopes
where new roads snake past the snowline
and the black amputated claws
of charred stumps
grip dirt in the scarcountry.

I have stumbled back to the woods
after drunken years of absence
driven again by several needs—
found my way to this woebegone place
of weatherbattered buildings
where a disused landing barge
landed forever
rusts in the bushes
like all my failed dreams.

Sing a song of recompense—
noisy joshing suppertimes
in a cookhouse with a broken guthammer.

Sing a song of necessity
in this ancient logging camp
by the tidal rapids called Skookumchuck
which means *strong water*
and must be drunk
beyond bottles.

Brawls

Breathless with delight
we see the grade-B western barrooms
erupt in the ersatz violence
of choreographed donnybrooks
balsawood chairs
splintering over hapless heads
candy windows smashing   the hero
swinging from handy chandeliers
to boot the badmen in the belly.

John Wayne and Randolph Scott
colliding like titans
trading merciless haymakers
each one enough to poleaxe an ox
yet up they jump unscathed
like tireless robots
to slug their way through Klondike dancehalls
in fistic marathons that end
with the foregone *coup de grâce*

and the slightly mussed victor
reeling back to the bar
for a manly shot of cold tea.

Young Broderick Crawford
walloping adversaries
with great meaty mitts
in southsea honkytonks,
Ward Bond's hulking renegade bully
challenged by slight Dana Andrews
grunting, "I'll get you, Logan!"
as a whiskey bottle breaks on his skull,
cocky James Cagney
toppling bullies twice his size
abandoning words for right hooks
in a backlot Hell's Kitchen—

William Bendix and Alan Ladd
battling side by side
an army of oriental thugs
in the alleys of a canvas Saigon.

How they tussle   tumble
toughtalk through our dreams
the named and nameless scufflers
of those bloodless set-tos
forgotten stuntmen of a sawdust universe
leaping valiantly from balconies
absorbing sometimes
more than imaginary punishment
for union scale
and the sake of our naive joy.

But one Saturday afternoon
in that boyhood pulpmill town
an old drunk comes to the matinee
to noisily annoy
the normally placid projectionist
until he loses control
drags the offender outside
administers a brutal battering
out of all proportion to his sins
leaves him lying there
like a groaning sack of garbage
giving the lie to Hollywood punch-ups
dribbling real-life unpretty gore
before our stunned and disillusioned eyes.

Overhead Crane

Insect-click of circuits
clang of struck steel
bells, buzzers, the vast orange bulk
of the building-wide crane
rumbling forward on charged rails
swinging its fat hook—
an electrified fisherman
of rivets, girders and grids.

In the Plexiglas box below its belly
I squat with my hands full of power.
I'm the brain of this robot—
it moves obedient to my whims,
lives at a lever's thrust—
I am its slave and its master.
Together we're an irresistible force,
strongest back in this potline.

Beneath our shadow the pots fume—
double row of giant conductors
riding on bathtubs of bauxite flux
juggling molecules into aluminum
alchemy on a mammoth scale—
enough voltage to light a small city
floods and hums here forever.
The air is acrid with smoke and ozone.

The pot-crews cough through the passages,
inferno-tenders in Stanfield shirts.
The line dwindles off to infinity.
Red and deadly, the magma bubbles
but I'm above and beyond all that,
safe in this plastic coccoon
breathing filtered air,
fishing for tubs of molten soup.

My robot and I ride herd on Hades
but it's lonely here at the top.
A machine's not much on conversation.
I'm trapped in an isolation booth,
I amuse myself with mad thoughts
like revving this beast up fullbore,
thundering down the monotonous tracks,
smashing clean through the wall to freedom.

Or running completely amok
charging off up the line
swinging my hook like a judgment
upsetting ore-trucks, braining foremen.
I'm God in a plastic box.
I've been in this smelter too long;
one of these shifts I'm just liable to do it.
Heads up, you bastards—it might be tomorrow!

The Cargo Hulks

Ramshackle barges
limp the coastal passages
carrying hogfuel and sulphur
to the ever-hungry mills—
food for the insatiable
bellies of the digesters,
ammunition for the smokestacks
to vomit at the gulls.

Cargo hulks
stripped of masts and superstructure—
name   rank   identity
any vestige of esteem,
they flounder through the waves
like great gutted whales
behind the strutting tugboats
and they dream

of full sail—
ferocious high seas thundering,
merciless Antarctic gales,
the howling challenge of the Horn,
shrouds under full stress bulging
like a trumpet player's cheeks,
the pitching—the nearly foundering,
the forging on

to dolphin country
in the long rolling heat
past stark coasts where volcanoes growl
like old men in beds—
equatorial becalments,
deckboards cracking in the sun,
parched voices croaking for a wind
on the hard green road.

Blowing north again
before a good kicking gust
through starsure climbing nights
new-minted days
to drop anchor at last,
winner of the harrowing marathon
before new-raised cabins smoking welcome
in the pioneer bays.

Memories melting
in the cold reality of rain
they wake to ultimate winters by wharves
in the overwhelming stink
become mere pawns
in the same industrial equation
that fouls the water brown and foaming
along their flanks.

The Dead Farm

Among those melancholy hills
the dead farm lives
ragged curtains
loll like grey tongues
from silent windows.

Relic of the high hollows
where they once read *Liberty*
in nineteen thirty-eight
western pulp magazines
yellowing in a shed
ancient religious tracts
long shredded by rats.

Stubborn they must have been
those vanished pioneers
settling to a scrub ledge
in a hardscrabble land.
The sadness of their thwarted venture
is told in weather-scuffed wood
sagging monuments of their labour
incline to the soil
antique automobiles rust
beyond the dry well
a half-buried ploughshare
lies where they left it.

Inside, forgotten clothes
hang where they hooked them
grimy bib overalls
a frayed greatcoat.
Upstairs, mouse droppings,
his going-to-meeting tie,
torn mattresses,
crumpled letters full of bad news.

They are forty years gone from their failure
in these bleak upland meadows
now we must follow their memories west
brushing the ghosts from our shoulders.

Deepcity Blues

Sunday cafe   beer on a tray
sandwiches nobody eats
tickets to drown in a bar-shuttered town
lonesome on butt-cluttered plates
refugees running from straitjacket rooms
searching for voices and booze
fulltime regretters who never get letters
desperate deepcity blues.

Johnny the booster is buying the drinks
with money he scored from his fence
for small nervous Sam from the Sally Ann
who worked on the waterfront once
for Billy the shot-to-hell sailor
who'll never swim back to the sea
for grey Frankie Fear who'll be dead in a year,
the dark, tarnished lady and me.

Orphan-sad people with no place to go
dreading the deepcity night
gripping this brief social moment
in the greasyspoon restaurant's light
clutching straw minutes with drowningman hands
gulping the straw-coloured beer,
me and the lady and Johnny and Sam
Billy and grey Frankie Fear.

Quicktalk and slicktalk and old broken dreams
scattered like cigarette ash
tabletop tales of cardcastle schemes
that always came down with a crash
Sally Ann Sam had a family once
but his children all act like he's dead
Grey Frankie Fear takes a swig of his beer
and repeats what the doctors have said.

Dark, tarnished lady is rubbing my leg
"Hey, honey, you got any weed?"
the joint's about folding   I tell her I'm holding
I've had all the booze that I need
we slip from that sad Sunday circle
the men who've paid too many dues,
to hide in the gloom of a straitjacket room
and smoke back the deepcity blues.

Deepcity blues   nothing to lose
lonelynight women who seldom refuse
Sunday cafes   casual lays
desperate deepcity blues.

York Hotel Elegy

In this block-wide grave
they are dismantling memories—
eyes gaze through fence peepholes,
jackhammers tommygun the dust,
dinosaur shovels
stuff dumptrucks full of yesterday—
the shock troops of progress
are proceeding as they must.

And I am climbing lost stairs
to vanished floors of frayed elegance
hand in hand with gentle Karen
in a season of regret.
In that ironic bridal suite
we toast the last hurrah of romance
count the disappearing fantasies
all the west-wheeling night.

There we sit in our naïveté
ten-cent philosophers
swapping half-truths in the half-light
of that halfway-house bar—
shapely Sherry steers her trayloads
through the smoke to thirsty tables,
old rounders eye her wistfully,
drown desires in their beer.

We exchange bad poetry
while the rest exchange racing tips
lies   goodbyes and slurry gossip,
selling tomorrow for a song.
How immutable it all seems
now only emptiness remains
a pit full of bricks and broken promises
that was waiting there all along.

The Slidingback Hills

The hills are sliding back
slipping into a distance
more profound than mere miles
floating into remoteness
down time's wrong-way telescope.

The hills are blurring bluely
into a land of spent winds   lost rains
sunken suns   shrunken snows
broken trees   broken friends
sounds of chaos shivering into silence.

Dark birds spin like wind-flung leaves
across an ice-pale sky
cold smoke of mist coils between the columns
of vanished virgin forests
phantom rigging crews
toil across torn slopes
and someone I once was
toils dimly with them
a prisoner of memory marooned
in a shadowy caulk-boot kingdom
trapped forever
among the slidingback hills.

Marble Arch

Two decades later in the same
room where I tried to kill myself
before caution was invented
I think of the brash clothes we wore
the skittish skindeep girls
we thought we wanted.

Familiar ghosts
slip unsummoned from the walls
move like puppets through their paces.
I'm always twenty here
popping caps from new bottles,
indulging timeworn vices.

In the bar's gloom I see
the careless friends I once knew
before we understood regret.
The new decor reverts
to its shabby oldtime look.
We trade the gossip of the street.

Tomorrow's long sword
has touched us with its shadow.
We pay it scant heed.
Oblivious with youth,
we know delusive immortality—
this now can never fade.

They have restructured the town
beyond our naive figments—
black towers grow haughty
from the graves of lost hangouts.
We wouldn't know ourselves from rubes
in this facelifted city.

Except in such fusty backwaters
as this overlooked hotel
they have not yet chosen to erase.
Here where a window called my foolish bluff
I talk abstractedly with phantoms,
am uneasily at peace.

The Others

There are sadder truths
beyond this safe Christmas
many men alone
and diminished women
crushed like flowers
between the pages of their pain.

In the country of rooms
there are no bright greeting cards
no presents in the mail
only ghostly ships in bottles
they can sail away on
sinking as they sail.

Desperately they seek
in wine seas of memory
a legacy less bitter
before time cut them adrift
and three wise men
fell dying in the gutter.

Deserted wives
morose in housing projects
and identical suites
unpack welfare hampers
among nagging children
in a season of defeat.

Haggard faces peer
from grubby lobby windows
of skidroad hotels
numb with unvoiced remorse
counting ghosts along the sidewalk
to the cynical bells.

At the City Mission
they dole out turkey dinners
for the price of a prayer.
The drifters make them last.
There's a week or more to welfare
and it's cold out there.

Snakey Jake
who's thirty-nine but looks sixty
gets bounced from a bar.
Undeterred, he finds a doorway
cracks a pint of rubby
takes a belt of Christmas cheer.

Merciful darkness
dusts down on the meanstreets
the many men alone
and the diminished women
crushed like flowers
between the pages of their pain.

Oldmother Jail

Farewell Oldmother Jail
you have shown me all
your pretty secrets.

I have flinched before the leers
of homosexual trusties
ogling us in entrance showers.

I have met lost friends
engulfed also
by your mouth of rotten-tooth laws.

I have heard a punchdrunk boxer
speak of old-time stir
with a curious nostalgia.

I have seen them bring the hookers
through from the women's unit,
recognized a junk-pinched face.

I have seen your handcuffed psychopaths
hustled roughly upstairs
to the observation tier.

I have seen the manacled pallbearers
bound for the institutional funeral
of a prison-perished crony.

I have seen the tittering queens
going gladly to the Pen
like kids to a candy store.

I have listened to the night talk
of your hamstrung and your doomed
like voices in some grim dormitory.

I have seen the pallid faces
of the men no one speaks to
pariahed on Death Row.

I have seen the green door
that leads to the hanging shaft
hidden in your heart.

I have seen your screws doing time
with your cons doing time
with your walls.

Farewell Oldmother Jail—
I leave you to your cages and your charges,
I leave you to your children.

The Ghosts

At the beginning of memory
the Clown crouches
doughnut lips
locked in a dreadful red smile
beckoning from corners
with banana fingers
grinning from fluid shadows
on upstairs evening landings
snickering beyond the night light
in bedrooms of bristling fear.

Too bewitched to resist
I move through deepest childhood
with phantoms no one else sees
clown   grey lady   black dog
sharing that house with the bricked-up room
where things scratch softly
that might be mice
books whisper in libraries
and in the spider-webbed attic
other-time artifacts twitch
like lavender cadavers
in mothballed leather coffins.

Trapped in the old enigma
I drift through the vague rooms
of the house that no one remembers
where one letter comes that is always black.

Once my father never came back
to that haven of omens
leaving only the echoes and shards of himself
for us who didn't need death so early.
My mother swore she heard the banshee
the night before his plane went down.
Her parents arrived within hours
to spirit us free of the clutching house.

The lesser ghosts thinned and subsided
but I saw my lost swing move to my father's hands.
That swing moves yet in my dreams
like a reckoning pendulum
and now my mother has joined him in the garden
by the haunted house at last
in the eternal youth of their broken love.

Ammonia Fumes

Night beyond night
I hid in sarcophagus bars
wearing futility like a placard,
declining my youth like Latin   declining
declining to face
the true scarred walls of limbo around me
the vague booze-flushed faces
mouthing street trivia at me through the smoke.

What would my English uncles have said—
those staid upstanding good and proper men
trotting their horses by the weirs
in green still-rivered fields
innocent of snakes or tomorrow's music—
to see me blacksheeping it so
living up to no expectations
but those of the bartender smiling his hard smile?

Night beyond night
I hid in sarcophagus bars
till sometimes the beer drowned me numb
and the waiter came with his small blue bottle.
Piercing ammonia fumes
stung the brain back from blackness
and I stumbled numbly away from the game.
They don't permit oblivion there.

A Wild Girl to Walk the Weathers With

for Yvonne

On bleak or blistering days
mountain-goating the hard tilting hills
in gaunt ice-carved valleys
slide-scarred,
headstoned with the high-notched stumps
of earlier invasions,
I fear no more the dancing deadly rigging
the sudden sidewinding logs
the hanging Babylonian slabs
for life has opened,
and I have at last
a wild girl to walk the weathers with.

In other camps, valleys, years,
I moved in terror between the lashing lines
and the not-loving,
the not-being-loved,
burned more deeply than the fear.

But though the hazards remain
ubiquitous as ever
they are endurable now
for life has opened
and I have at last
a wild girl to walk the weathers with.

Summer Microcosm

Tethered by two clotheslines
the house hangs moored in the garden,
green waves beat
on the grey-white hull of its walls.

In the silver maple
hot wind turns the powdered leaves
like flashing fingers drumming
against the sun.

Goldfinch on the fencepost
stands like a pillar saint—
his penance is brief—
he sparks off down a breeze.

Small red eyes in the raspberry bushes
are only specks of summer blood,
waiting for quick hands or beaks
to wipe them away.

Tiny orange fragment
of nervous muslin:
a butterfly takes inventory
among the fevered roses.

Stocky late cornstalks
flap leathery pinions,
straining like buried birds
to wrench triumphant from the soil.

The peach tree
fashions his sugar-balls slowly—
we will catch before they drop
their sweet gold of continuance.

The apple tree
dying of apathy and caterpillars
puts forth a few sour fruit
small and bitter as tears.

Hot enough to cook slugs—
they lurk glutinous in leafcaves
hallucinating rain,
plotting fresh outrage on cabbages.

A man looking long enough
might fall out through his eyes,
lose himself quick as a sandgrain
in the coarse grass.

In the busy green sea of the garden
the house tugs at its moorings,
mundane ark
of whatever we must wake to.

Stronghold of All She Was

In memory of my mother

In the melancholy heat
the house is limned with whispering light
the neglected garden jungles up
stubborn flowers she planted   burgeoning weeds.
Nothing is the same or will be ever.
The steady hands are still.

The gentle ever-busy hands
are gone from her cottage by the sea
the house she dreamed of, found and made happy
her last small kingdom of kindness
the final fertile refuge of her days
breached by dark wings.

Her sculptures still hang from wall and ceiling
her paintings rejoice in their frames
the novel she never finished dreams in a drawer
her character smiles from every corner.
But the old armchair is empty
the kitchen waits in vain for her singular touch.

She will not be back
there was too much joy in her to conjure a ghost
and I know she is at peace anyway
that small vital woman who wished no one ill.
Thus I shall live in the warmth of her good memory
and haunt this house duly in her stead.

A Ticket to Ramsay Arm

for Jack Williams

One slackassed spring
I picked up a hiring-slip from a mancatcher in a bar
told him I'd fly up the following day
guy was so tickled he fronted me twenty bucks.

I had more good intentions than a Sally Ann street preacher
but with all that moolah, I ran a little amok
found a lot of beer   a bottle   a broad
missed the goddamn plane.

Well, I kicked myself a bit over that one
played the duck for the mancatcher
felt like sixteen kinds of a drunken fool
till I read the evening paper.

Seems like half a bloody mountain
had slid down on the camp I was bound for
bulldozed the cookshack into the sea
buried the rest of it, killed five men.

One of those poor stiffs could have been me!
That was about the only time
drinking ever handed me more
than a sore head and a bad reputation.

The Guests

Around our wilderness mountaintop table
the guests begin to gather
an incursion of the small
chittering twittering closer
circling through the sun-circled afternoon.

Like fencers they advance and retreat
wary eyes take our measure
prudently they hesitate
but the lure of the crumbs proves too strong
their forest caution deserts them.

Quick squirrels dart to the booty
whisky-jacks filch from our fingers
a tiny stouthearted chipmunk
scales the ramp of my hand
with thistledown feet and attains the prize.

It is a scene out of St. Francis of Assisi
a nature film by Walt Disney
the small have offered their trust
and we are the guests   not they
scattering our tithes in a highcountry clearing.

The Beginning Again

Ironic cackle of a duck
derisive in the dawn
waves like whispering explosions
along the shore
boats stuttering alive
hungry to hit the fishward trail
time beginning again
for them   for us.

Greek chorus of awakening
cats piteous at the door
one single distant dog bark
your soft still half-dreaming voice
incredibly discreet creak
of the mattress as we embrace
time clicking the switches back on
for us   for them.

This secret scenario
was thus since God first cast the dice
it is the miracle of recommencing
after our little deaths in the darkness
it is mortality's song
orchestrated before sunrise
it is the simple hymn of re-being
the beginning again.

Mist Above the Memories

for Geoff and George

High country   cold August
steep uptrudge from the road's-end river
panting with the pack-weight
beside the ruined tramway
past the dam   the intake-keeper's cabin
climbing leadenly through virgin timber
to the low snowline
where tree-islands thrust from unmelted drifts
rotting stumps like the thrones of strange mountain kings.
Beartracks   goattracks   legs like rubber
stumbling endlessly up the white ridges
exhaustedly into the gaunt valley
making camp by a frozen lake
bloodstained with red algae
drinking glad by a twilight fire
coffee, rum and soup on a rocky outcrop
lying sleepless at last in a blue tent
in the chill dense silence.

Four thousand feet below
Woodfibre's mill belches poison still
among the wreckage of the phased-out townsite:
abandoned cars in collapsing garages
buckled children's slides   gone-wild gardens
drunk ghosts in the decertified Legion
phantom rumble of tenpin balls in stripped alleys
pokergame bunkhouses bulldozed to splinters
lost loved women of twenty years back
confronting middle age in other places
brief friends of youth scattered forever
to the grey winds   only the factory left
in the ruck of the ruined community
for commuting workers to visit.

The fog blurs up around us, blotting the moon
I'm tired as a run hound but I can't sleep
the images persist
there's no time here on this shrouded mountain.
Somewhere the town still exists.

The Carnival Comes to Kitimat

Canvas flaps in the field below the smelter
roustabouts shuffle and spit
dubious women emerge from trailers
a withered geek stands scratching his crotch
light rain splashes on faded frescoes
there are grunting sounds from tarpaulined cages
scuffed wooden horses are tethered to rides
mallets thud on tent pegs
a cigar-chewing fat man barks orders
a small bedazzled dog sits watching.
We stand watching with him—
anything's news in this goddamn town.

Night rides in on a cold valley wind
the fairground throbs with colour
the Ferris wheel winds its squealers aloft
barkers rattle staccato lies
hot-dog vendors dispense indigestion
a fortune teller dispenses vague guesses
tawdry prizes are occasionally won
children goggle in seventh heaven
their parents goggle inwardly.
We're all sitting ducks for the hucksters—
anything's news in this goddamn town.

In the stripper's tent   Adults Only
an aging blonde shakes to a scratchy record
grunts and snickers
"Put it on for God's sakes!" shouts someone
it's more pathetic than erotic
mechanically she shrugs through a bump-and-grind
her face is a desperate mask of pancake makeup

and suddenly I realize I know her,
see the unravaged face ten years forgotten.
I duck for fear she might see me
flee the tent and the fifth-rate tinsel gayway
the past like a knot in my gut—
anything may be news in this goddamn town
but this kind of news I can do without.

The Lowest-Paid Job in the Woods

The whistlepunk I was staggers
up muddy hills in a rattle of rain
uncoiling as he climbs
a heavy noose of wire, umbilical lengths
trailing away behind, across the canyon
to the slave-driving mother machine.

The rest of the crew's pulling strawline
so nobody's getting off easy
except the engineer
and at least my load lightens
with every black coil I throw away.

Come at last to a likely vantage point
I scale a cedar stump and sit
smoking   sweating   hearing
the raindrops bounce from the duck's-back rubber—
I'm wetter than hell anyhow.

They're rigged up and it's starting time.
Someone shrieks like a goosed owl.
I press the wooden dingus in my fist—
the horn cries   the engineer hits his levers
the choked logs leap to life
thrash and batter down the slope
to the spar-tree.

Between shouted signals
I dream of songs and stories—
think of the legendary whistlepunk
back in the Dirty Thirties
whose partner was killed on the rigging
by a production-crazy foreman—
who stayed on in camp, waited his chance
caught the foreman in the bight
blew the wrong whistle, let the logs take him
blamed a raven, sailed away
proving vengeance
is not solely the province of heaven.

They call me a *whistlepunk* derisively
I must endure
the stinging tradition of their scorn
when daily I hold their lives, like mice,
at the mercy of my fingers.

Annie of the Corridors

Madonnas of the fogged past
you move through endless passageways
interminable rooms
constant among the transience
of transient hotels:
aging hennaed women with much English,
pretty Slavic girls with little—
Betty   Olga   Doris   Petruska
and the nervous one with the unpronounceable name.

Lost ladies of morning halls
like displaced mothers   amnesiac sweethearts
triggering vague dreams
of love or guttering lust
in the drifting minds of lonely men.

Annie of the corridors,
queen of the Marble Arch chambermaids,
how I imagined I loved you
in the pinched and alienated days
when nothing like love seemed likely again.

Annie of the fine roan hair,
the full proud man-familiar body,
the fortyish worldwise sensual face,
you ran your troops like a no-nonsense madam
and my fantasies like a succubus.

Annie, my seamstress of dreams
who once sewed two buttons on my one shirt
after a drunken scuffle,
who sometimes shared a beer with me
but never my bed.

Annie, immovable Annie
rejecting my clumsy advances,
telling me with enormous finality:
"You're young enough to be my son.
And you drink too much."

Annie, empress of linen closets
in visions, I stride surely back to you
no longer a boy or drunk   King of the Janitors
with coveralls and an amorous moustache.
We are made for each other   we make love
in all the empty rooms,
are married by the Manager
and rule that dusky corridor empire forever.

Landslide Daffodil
for Barbara Williams

Log boom snails through the gap
on a blowing blue day
among the salmon skiffs
sailboats knifing white and faster
before the bird-flecked breeze
powerboats lunging north
on featherpaths of foam.

Waves lick distantly
wooded islands beyond
far clouds scroll the horizon
over unfenced Pacific
on slow Sunday sitting
shorebound amid shushing
tidesounds   voices
in the warm vault of spring
tickling lazy words
in counterpoint   thinking
windthoughts.

Rising, I walk
a teredo-mined log
more holes than wood
climb buckled stairs
that lead to nowhere now
but the heart of an old landslide
beneath a raw clay cliff
pick the lone daffodil
that thrusts from the ruck
of a runaway garden
carry it back
to a girl who couldn't love me
even for sunshine
or the soft day's sake.

Moon Song

This night the world is mine and the moon's
peering like a pale egg yolk
through a porthole of pushing cloud
cratered globe of space-battered stone
hypnotist's watch
unleashing madmen   awakening werewolves
tugging the tide up like wet sheets
you're open for business, ball of myths.

Christmascard trees, black in your brittle light
backdrop my ramshackle hideaway
you're a scarred yellow pool ball
cued and rolling forever across night's table
you're the pockmarked pusher
peddling dreams in dusk-clotted alleys.
I'll buy your wares, old brother
anything's better than earthbound lies.

You are my heart gone sick from the universe
raddled rock lantern of ungranted wishes
sun-muscles twitch you golden
we throb to the same dim principle
all birds   all trees   all beasts and people,
only God knows the rhyme or reason.
He lets you shimmer on like a beacon
and lets me shiver on like a fool.

The Eastend Toronto Railroad Insomnia Blues

All night long on Boultbee Street
the boisterous trains shudder past
from every continental direction.
The bones of the house bounce with their passing
jolting me countless cursing times
back from the brink of sleep
to lie like a beached fish
in high-and-dry wakefulness, gasping for dreams.

I've been spoiled too long by country silence.
This is like stretching out in a bowling alley
where some mad league plays forever
on lanes of sheet metal with cannonballs.
Since I'm scarcely allowed to forget them
I think of trains and their predicted decline—
chuffing, shunting, piston-throbbing
over tired tracks to weedy extinction.

Whoever believes in such balderdash
should spend a few nights in this besieged room—
something's sure out there alive and kicking
up merry hell in the thunderstruck dark.
My brother's got a soft spot for trains
(maybe that's why he bought this house),
rode the rods east here when he was sixteen
ate rotten pork chops with hoboes in sandhouses
froze on gondolas in northpole winds
almost went under the wheels once
a hair's breadth away from a legless beggar—
he spoke of it almost fondly tonight
as whiskey adventured him back.

I have come better late than never
to this musclebound city too big for its boots
low by a windy lake
with only tall buildings and towers for mountains.
It is a time for remembering
for tossing sleepless in bed
hearing the hotshot freight trains earthquake by
like the runaway years.

Through the Apricot Air

A poet is dreamfooted and walks a curious tightrope
his song rises strangely through the apricot air
love is his joy   his tool   his wisdom   his folly
he circles mothlike the candleflame truth of things.

He strikes from nothing the sparks of what ought to exist
the knowledge aches out of his eyes   creation's his purpose
he scrawls on the sky   inhabits the lunatic corners
in the web of delusion he crouches, alert as a spider.

A poet is a decoder of arcane messages
received on the crystal set of his eavesdropping heart
from the scrabble-bag of letters he plucks the singing images
threads them like beads on the lines of his secret longing.

He is a cardsharp of words that sting and praise and wonder
his mind swings erratically between micro and macrocosm
he studies the eccentric comings and going of house finches
and the ghostly pillars that whelp stars at the edge of the universe.

A poet is a brief mad seer in a sea of bottomless mysteries
he is driven more by curiosity than wisdom
he lives his life by luck, intuition and chance
and leaves as his legacy only a random scattering
of delirious verse.

Drunkwalk

Like a molasses-footed man in a dream
down a hill of all my years and staggerings
taking wrong turnings
down dead-end roads on dead legs
humpty-dumpty drunk
pitching in ditches   tearing my coat
only the moon mocking down
a sideways yellow smirk in the murky sky
past cop-shops and gone-to-bed houses
instinct pushing me on like a pilot light
dim glimmer somewhere under the suds and wine
no woman   no friend   no sense
sing a song of slewfooted stumblebums
I have found the enemy and he is me
this bald spent guzzler reeling homeward
all the evening's aimless conversations
chattering like magpies in broken branches of memory
all the ramblings of all the poured-away nights
rattling down the past in diminishing echoes
I guess I'll never learn   never learn   never learn
there is nothing this way but the little death of oblivion
I seek from old habit years beyond the need
drunkwalk through a blurred snoring town
two timeless hours past meaningless midnight
to lurch at last through the door of my cage
and bed down blind in my clothes like an overdue corpse.

Sifting the Debris

I am sifting the debris of several lifetimes
in this sold shell of a house
this womb of memories and crumbling wood
where I have coiled like a foetus
for too many years.

Ghosts of old songs   lost circumstances
drift through the room like winter breath
I have breathed smoke and sorrow here
laughter, too   confused love
of girls who were mostly mistakes
and one who wasn't—
of a small loyal mother
who killed me with kindness
raised me to poems
and vanished forever,
of brothers who burned by the wayside
and climbed from their ashes,
of friends, also brothers,
who bootstrapped to betterment   of friends
who put guns in their mouths
jumped from bridges and windows
walked up lonely valleys with noosed ropes
passed like sad echoes.

Phantom cats
lie curled on window ledges of recollection
like mongrel shades they haunt
this sagging mansion of other days—
from incomprehensible distances
their trusting paws reach out
their small voices speak to me yet.

This house where once I retied
a psychic umbilical cord
and made a shaky pact
with alcohol and words,
reaches out beyond me into time
each invisible finger
a conduit to another yesterday
and all the yesterdays before my birth—
my mother safe in Malayan girlhood,
my father biplaning over the Himalayas,
my grandfather deciphering Greek in his study,
my grandmother tending kitchen and gardens.

And all the forebears before them
indistinct legends dwindling into history.

I am sifting the detritus
of much more than myself
in this dusty focal point
where a long phase is stumbling
to a final halt—an obscure epoch
stuttering into silence.

I relinquish custody
of this museum house and its relics—
collapsed portal to the past,
rotted afterbirth of dreams.

Hell's Gate

At Hell's Gate that great wallow of water
a million gallons of ramming thrust
squeezes through the canyon's narrowest throat
in a tumbling thunder
of foam and elemental fury.

Once history ran rampant
as the river between these cliffs
headless armless miners
swam its grim flood
in the goldrush massacres
and the gallant paddleboat *Scuzzy*
battled its way uptorrent against all odds
and the current.

An even century later
I swallow my acrophobia and ride
that spidery tramcar with you
over and down to the gorge's bottom.
Here where explorers
once gnawed on pemmican
we breakfast on bacon and eggs.
The hounds of hell have been brought to heel
and the legends reduced
to expensive books in the souvenir shop.

Early Shift

At 4:30 AM
by the ghostly gas station
a piece of silver paper
wind-scratching across the asphalt
is a noisy insect for the nerves.

I wait, unwillingly awake
with only a gutcan, a cigarette
and random thoughts for company.
The cops are all asleep with their guns.
The town lies ripe for the taking.

But I haven't a burglar's belly.
I'll help steal trees instead
from a hill that's warming up for me now.
By noon that bitch'll be hot enough
to make the devil sweat blood.

Across the last stars
three puny cloud-threads crawl.
Not a whisper of rain in those timid drifters.
They'll scatter like scared dogs
when the haymaker comes up.

It's time. Inescapably the crummy
trails its headlights
through the locked village
come to shanghai me once more
to a clockwork mountain.

Requirements

All I need
is a yellow cat coming home
like sunlight
through the dying year's grey
after three days missing to know
this ticklish world continues
though bony fingers poke
through my pockets and yours.

All I need
is a more-than-curious girl
descending time's elevator
to the floor of my life to know
this slippery world proceeds
though keeper eyes watch always
through the peepholes of our hearts.

And all I need
is another dream to bend right
in the random direction
of a better poem
to scratch on these prison walls and know
this murky world reinvents itself
though white jaws grinning forever
ring all our campfires like wolves.

The Dream Shift

Two seaplanes pull their sounds
across the Sound
above this logrobber's land
against a pale sky
to somewhere north of my inertia
perhaps a wave-slapped dock
where half a crew's quit for the hell of it
and waits with caulk boots tied to their baghandles.

Two seaplanes pull my mind
through cobweb walls
to where I left my last bad woodsdream
wetly quivering:
all the worst sidehills of my life
become one impossible panorama,
a thousand riggingmen anting across it,
a hundred haywire donkeys thundering above them.

Everything but the kitchen sink
is charging downmountain on those poor bastards—
it's hell's own bowling alley
with a lot of dancing damnfools for pins.
I'm both above and among them
both dodger and watcher
caught in the bight of my fantasies,
feeling the rush of remembered adrenalin.

Behind the lines like an armchair general
I hear the distant battlecrash
and run the hills I rebuild in the night
in camps I can never quit.

The Last Spar-Tree on Elphinstone Mountain
for Al Purdy

The last spar-tree on Elphinstone Mountain
through drunken-Sunday binoculars
pricks the blue bubble of the sky
on that final ridge where the scar tissue peters out.

Been four years quiet now on the battered mountain's back
except for shakecutters, hunters and stray philosophers.
The trucks are elsewhere; some of the drivers dead
and the donkeys gone to barber another hill.

I'm always shooting my mouth off about mountains
sometimes climbing them
and sometimes just distantly studying them like this.
My eyes need no caulk boots
I can vault to that ridge in my mind,
stand at the foot of that tree, forlorn as a badly used woman
become merely landmark and ravenperch.
I can touch its bark sunwarm as flesh
feel the engines still shaking it functional
with vibrations that never quite die.

It's either a cornfield or a catastrophe.
Either a crop or a tithe or a privacy
has been taken from this place.
What matter? It's done. Beyond that ridge is a valley
I helped hack and alter. There's a gully there
three hundred feet deep in places
where we tailholted on its rim.
Dizzy abyss that scared the wits out of me
you furrow down the mountain like God's own drainage ditch
and stopped a forest fire in 1965.

At your foot is the dirtiest show of them all
where we logged in the box canyon with debris crashing down
and the rotten hemlock snags trembled over us,
the haulback stumps pulled out like bad teeth.
The hooktender said: "She's a natural-born bitch!"
The lines broke—the omens spoke
and I quit from fear to become a brief boomman.

I'm getting melodramatic again but it's hard not to.
Logging's larger than life. Keep your sailors and cowboys!
I'm always stressing the sombre side
but there was much of comradeship and laughter—
great yarns beside noon donkeys; hillhumour between turns,
excellent shits behind stumps with the wind fanning the stink away,
sweat smelling good and cigarette smoke celestial.

Dream on in peace, old tree—
perhaps you're a truer monument to man
than any rocktop crucifix in Rio De Janeiro.

Serpentine Fen

Pocket of beauty locked between parallel highways
fringed by farmfields—
protected marsh with the sinuous name
chittering with birdsong under the sun.

Serpentine River, true to its calling
snakes across the northern margins
silty oceanic channel, toothed with oysters
flooding coffee-coloured below the dike.

This is an avian Eden now
a metropolis of bulrushes
where small things flit through seed-rich aisles
celebrating summer's rebirth.

Red-winged blackbirds crimson the thickets
a trusting mother duck parades her brood
swallows loft to nests in rickety lookout towers
killdeer glide like brown phantoms over the dike path.

Larger birds throng the southern reaches
families of geese flotilla the quiet sloughs
great blue heron   aloof   inscrutable
stands guard among a cluster of tiny islands.

The frail old man of the marsh
perennial watcher of Serpentine Fen
reclines on a shooting stick
blue-veined hands clutching a high-powered telescope.

His failing eyes are intent
as he studies the bird-busy swamp—
ancient amid the joy   the regeneration
he savours this yearly ritual.

"Two California avocets are nesting here
for the first time," he quavers
alight with the wonder of it   and somehow
that small marvel seems far more significant
than all the crimes and crises
that yammer hysterically forever
beyond this sanctuary.

Day to Day Blues

And there are always
new hills to climb
which are the same damn hill
wearing different men
and wearing them down.

Yesterday I worked in rain
with the flu virus
working in me
and tore up more territory
to the hollow music of money.

Dripped home in the evening
and changed identity
to sniffle in a baronial living room
a most unliterary guest
as they clicked the coloured words.

Out in the morning
to blizzard winds and shutdown.
Back to a letter from lucky Karen
in warmwicked Jamaica,
and a vicarious mickey of therapeutic rum.

We Measure the Miles in Muffets

Laughing our way through Wisconsin
we measure the miles in muffets
for so you have christened the hay bundles
that throng the mown fields
as though newly tumbled
from some celestial cereal box in the sky.

Round and perfect as yellow cheeses
they stock the pastures
dwindling into the distance
to become dime-sized in remote farmlands
benign and cheerful in sunlight
sinister somehow at twilight
like great waiting wheels
ready to roll upon us.

How we disparage the drab spreads
where the hay is bundled in mundane rectangles
or piled in loaves like so much bread.
Only the muffets win our approval
like old friends   happy omens
they guide us across the top of America.

Bending up out of Montana
through ugly towns with beautiful names
Sweetwater   Sunburst
we cross the line and find to our pleasure
more of our mute companions—
the muffets have trundled to Canada too.

Now in a bright niche of memory
the muffets shine like gold coins
a currency of droll magic
that brought us a bushel of wonders
in the fall of a travelling year
in the warm fall of our lives.

Progress Report
for Malcolm Lowry

These hills are browner and less
than when you penned them alive
in a sea-slapped shack
in the name of wonder and fear
when you wrote the gulls from the wind
caught the gist of the tide
called down sunsets to hang
in your dreams when your eyes were here.

With a book   a bottle of gin
clutched like weapons you walk
toward that long-ago lens,
a vision-tormented squatter
now just an ironic plaque
on a public toilet remains
the pier   the cabin are gone
the world grows older   no better.

The woods grow thinner   the deer
slip wary through what is left
the bears are wormy with garbage
the squirrels store poisoned nuts
Hell has expanded and spread
the city gobbles the green
the air is fetid   the fishermen
trap tainted fish in their nets.

Old wizard of words who clung
to this place with a desperate love
who drank your genius dry
when the world was a few years cleaner
your portents smoulder to truth
the restive volcanoes smoke
a judgment growls in the ground
the demons slink from the corner.

The King of Rhymes and Whistles

for Robert Swanson

Doggerel hero, spurred on by Bob Service,
your ballads banged through my boyhood.
Rough House Pete Olesen rampaged through my mind—
the Big Swede Logger gallumphed through my dreams.
The woods you described were a storybook place,
a northern Old West with loggers for cowboys,
a larger-than-life world of caulk-booted tough guys
storming the hills like Paul Bunyan's children.

Time had its way and I came to the jungles,
laced my first caulks on and stumbled to battle,
found that your woods kingdom had a few drawbacks—
bugs, hellish weather and wall-to-wall danger.
I stuck with the racket, too foolish to quit,
shrugged off the punches and found my own poems
but the loggers had yours by heart, Bob Swanson.
You were their king of rhymes and whistles.

Many years after, we sat on a stage
telling our poems and stories together.
You, the old trouper   me, the rank upstart
stirring the memories, stoking the legends.
Now you've hired out to those Holy Ghost camps
with a rucksack of myths, a suitcase of echoes
leaving a boy in an aging man's body
still hearing your whistles and heeding your rhymes.

Cinderwind

When the cinderwind's breath
blew my valley black,
the sky was a fevered flush
full of singed crows
and the quick green death.

Sap-factories exploding
the trees went up like hair
on a torched woman.
Along the awakened air
the flayed smoke came riding.

Among stampeded machines
below we watched
the gallivanting flames
graffiti the captured hill
with demented designs.

And the cinderwind whipped
a frenzy of glow-worms
to the distant echoing stars
in a cackle of abandon
as the day dipped.

Till it reined at the gully
that cut like a mortal wound
down the stump-chimneyed slopes,
barred by its dripping abyss
from the outer valley.

Foiled in a snort of sparks
it paced the damp edges
licked the unpalatable rocks
hissed like a dying god
to the hard dark.

Kicking through eaten ash
of smouldering aftermath
we hunted its stubborn remnants
with spitting canvas snakes
in the sunflash.

Cold snow will accrue
to bandage the savaged earth
in medical winter
to hide the dust-clotted scars
where the cinderwind blew.

Garden Music

Music in the garden,
pure cry of flowers—
I am ringed with wise colour,
August chords of tint
singing out to the universe—
one dark red Stravinsky rose
magnificently conducting
golden horns of the marigolds,
harps of flesh-pink phlox,
mauve cellos of the daisies,
reeds of purple-yellow pansies,
pastel violins of the fading hydrangeas.

I hide from the heat
this orchestrated afternoon
crouching drowsy
in the shadecave of the dying summer lilacs,
the bony laburnum with its poisonous pods
thinking of a girl with sunwarm skin
I kissed before she left
and will kiss again,
who is part of the music of this day—
this throbbing dark beneath the bushes
where I listen to the garden playing
arrangements of rocks and grass.

The Outer Island

There were times when the water lathered and leapt
lurched and crashed through the gap
barring us from the island.
We had tried it once when the weather frowned
bucked till we lost the prop
and wet white fingers drummed us back to the mainland.

So we went there only on diamond days
when the sea arched soft to the sun,
beached in a cove of tree chunks,
slashed our way through the braiding brush
to the hush of the island's heart,
traced our invisible lines between bluffs and tree trunks.

Through hoary jungles of high salal
we whittled with saw and knife
the transit findings to mark us,
pounded plugs in the rain-pecked rock,
hammered stakes in the earth,
learned the land and carved it up like a carcass.

In the last lax hours, we walked the shore,
sprayed our names on a cliff,
pictured the coming hordes of town-vacators.
Our thoughts blew south on a cynic's wind,
we gunned the outboard for home
and left an island betrayed to the speculators.

Writer's Block on Soames Hill

Beside you on the rim
of the moss-thatched summit
we have attained gasping
this evening of impulses,
I strain too hard for poetry
see only a village
sprawled in a crook of land
last sunlight splashing
golden from windows
to join in a giant jellyfish form
on the flat bay perhaps
some other whimsical time   tonight
only light
the mountains
only mountains
the boats
simply boats   no images   they won't
come when you try to force them
but lie dormant   things
are as they seem   no more.

Later descending
that deadsteep trail
reflective among the bony trees
feeling old logger muscles
work in my legs
first time in years,
I clasp you when I can
kiss you when we clasp my
soft girl of strangenesses
whose defences melt easily
to the proper heat
melt as we move
downmountain to the car
to whatever we must
perhaps a tender magic
better than the poem
I reached for to no avail
on eaglerocks with vistas
too vast for grasping.

Hoodoo Cove

Gaunt buildings beckon
beyond a dripping wall of alders
draw me up a tangled trail
to stand before a doorless bunkhouse
so enormous
the farther end of its corridor
is only a tiny rectangle
of rain-polished light.

I move toward it and enter
boots tapping ghosts awake
in the mildewed rooms
with their rusty iron bedsteads
empty window sockets
breached ceilings weeping water.

A decomposing dartboard
hangs limp and pitted
on a central wall.
Dimly I hear lost laughter
the careful thuds of evening contests
but the loggers are thirty years gone.

Four hundred men
worked this outfit once
until a plague of teredos
drilled the booms to trash.
After only three years
the site was abandoned.

Back at the beach, the log-dump
its planks pulpy with age—
its donkey engine
corroding on a moss-furred platform
like a forgotten idol—
points shakily across the bay
where an Indian handlogger
last inhabitant of this unlucky place
moves distantly
like a prophecy
against the sinister green trees.

The Language Keeper

for Louis Miranda

Time has distilled his essences
to a small scant-wrinkled brown man
with astute glittering eyes
telling of long-gone lacrosse teams
potlatches   chiefdom   the sons   the singing
his father forging through treacherous seas
north from the Inca south to sire him.

Chilean blood
and the blood of cedar-bark shamans
mingle in him.
A child of coupled cultures
his lineage links two continents.
But his loyalties lie with this place
homeland of his mother
viridian sprawl of mountains   inlets   islands
and lodgepole villages empty under the rain.

Amid the clutter of a lifetime
in the small drab house on the North Shore reserve
his talk turns to longshoring days
all the remembered workmates
Tango Dan   The Terrible Turk
sweat   calamity   laughter
in hard holds of the past.
The incredibly gentle voice
caresses the gritty memories
like the slim long-ago girl
his shy huge wife must have been
when he first went down to the lumber ships.

Those were a young man's labours.
In latter years he has found more rewarding work—
proudly he takes down the books from their special shelf.
He has transcribed the Squamish tongue
captured its unwritten cadences
in two life's-work volumes.
Those vanishing gutturals and sibilants
that echo faintly in forest-drowned places
will not now be forgotten.

The dark face lights in the good knowledge of it.
He has met the test of his dream.
We share his quiet content in the dim room.

Logger's Rain

The kind of soft autumn rain
it was good to work in the woods in
tickles from a tarnished sky
the roof of my idle cover—
trickles from the hard-hat rims
of all my peers and successors
who slog the stumpslopes yet
on the mountains I've fled forever.

Almost two years since I lost
my last caulk boots on purpose
my torn rainclothes too
and the gloves just one day worn
slung them under the crummy seat
for next year's greenhorns to find
laughed through the shutdown snow
free as a sprung con.

Destiny's punk in a dream
aboard that last-time boat
I blew strange smoke in the backseats
with the new-way forest kids
watched by amused old fallers
bound for the Hastings' hotels
the familiar skidroad sabbaticals
in their hoarded holiday duds.

Quit three times but this one's for real
I'll never go back, not ever,
except in my mind to the chokers
the hillsweat, the game you can't win.
But it's two years later. The rain falls
down the homesick sky like a memory
the kind of soft autumn rain
it was good to work in the woods in.

A Music Against Midnight

In the house with the broken heart
the ancient woman
lives like a brown ghost
bowed   shuffling   birdfrail
a stubborn survivor
brave at the brink with her memories.

She is badgered by time but her eyes
still clear, float like berries
in crinkled sockets
as she toasts her ninety-fourth year
with two medicinal bottles of beer each morning
to ease the tremulous decline.

For a dollar a day and breakfast,
I watch over her life's spare winter
in this backwater place where the clocks have frozen
back in the breadline Thirties
and the echoing talk of long-dead relatives
hangs in the halls among the shadows.

Sometimes in the nervous night
I ready speeches for phantoms
tense in my ticking room
but there is only the small sound of mice
industrious between the walls
and the old woman worrying through her dreams.

But sometimes she plays the piano
when beer has loosened arthritic fingers
and as I listen in a sad and speechless wonder
she bridges the gulf beyond reckoning,
sends the defiant anthems of her youth
rallying through the rooms.

Outport

Setting sun alchemizes
sluggish concertina waves
by slag-black islands
and rotting piers
that crawl like headless centipedes
into the sea to die.

Man is only
a memory of vanished voices
his fireplaces offer only cold ash
to a smoke-lonely sky
his fishboats have fled
from the shadow-fishing shore
his nets rot like huge webs
in sheds of jealous spiders.

He has become his empty bottles
his rust-mottled tins
his rained-away footprints
his inarticulate newspapers
peeling from articulate walls
his wife's weather-shredded dress
his children's toys
only pack rats play with now
his net racks   his artifacts   his ruins.

He has left this outport behind him
like his forgotten sou'wester
only his wistful dreams
live here sometimes.

The silver shade of a boy
pushes a phantom dory
across the wet pebbles
rows the accordion-pleated sea
toward the slag-black islands.

The Dams and the Dynamos

Until the poles and the powermen topple
there will be red energy under the eggs
fireflies to fire the bulbs
flickering ghosts in hypnotic boxes
fans to tickle us cool
thermostat heaters to wake us warm
music plucked from the air
until the dams and the dynamos break.

We have become too at ease with ease—
we suck the lazy electric tit
our homes are dependent husks
only bought lightning prickles alive.
We hide in sizzling cities
with factories that conveyor us fat
screens full of demon lovers
shrewd computers that audit our souls.

And when the cord severs sometimes
in truthblack winters in storms, we curse
through dark with the cold mounting
down to candles and uncertain batteries.
If the outage persisted, we'd set
trueflames in our plastic fireplaces
beg the atrophied knacks
but always the power returns again.

Until the dams and the dynamos break
we will hibernate in complacent caves
watching the lost of the world
shiver and die in swamp and desert.
We will sorrow or simply shrug
the acknowledged children of affluence
till the lights go dead   for good
and thin hands smash
through our privileged windows.

In the Gully

In the dripping gully
the spider-rooted windfall
sucks up under the granite lip
of the overhang
and stops.

Thumb the button
of the electric belt-whistle
I wear like a six-shooter
confident the haulback line
will jerk the jammed wood free,
but it doesn't.

Go ahead on the mainline again.
Cable grinds against stone
to no avail. The windfall
lies locked in the ravine.

Glance at my chokermen—
they gaze back blankly.
Not their problem,
only and incontestably mine.

Go ahead once more.
The mainline sings to parting point.
Hit the whistle again
at the last grating moment.

Back slams the windfall
but this time
there is just enough slack
to unhook the choker.

Leave it there thankful, thinking
logging's a lot like writing poetry.
Mind-cables wrench loose
the stubborn ideas,
sometimes to wedge them
in hopeless canyons
and knowing just when
to blow the whistle and cut them off
is a knack
of no small importance.

A Small Hum of Joy in the Heart

for Yvonne

In the prickly darkness
I prowl the rim of consciousness
tracking a lost sensibility
hidden behind the forebrain
in thickets of memory—
twisting away   disappearing
around blind corners of the cortex.

I spin through dither and dream
to the ghostplace
where poems once shivered alive—
tingled and twitched   initiating
a small hum of joy in the heart.

I scrabble back
to old creative days
when the good poems danced with the bad
in prolific confusion,
splashed in the pools of my being,
coddled in the blithers,
whistled in the fiff—
gibberish of undecoded poetry
before it became poetry
shrugging itself lucid,
forming itself into ranks,
marching away to the fingertips.

But the poems sift slow now   infrequently,
the fluency has forsaken me,
the sturdiest verses were nurtured in loneliness—
perhaps love has bred a complacency.

Love is a lotus song   an exquisite lunacy—
a sorcery dressed in rosepetals,
a fond interlocking   a twinning,
 a small hum of joy in the heart.

Have I lost the poems to love?
Unlikely   but even if so
it has been a healthy exchange—
a passing of pain   a tender completion.
I shall never regret it.

Harrison Hot Springs Nocturne

Snow wind whistles
from high muffled peaks
tourist town crouches
on the rim of dark waters
achingly remote
lighthouse blinks wanly
steam wreathes the sulphur springs
like ghosts of fur traders.

Laughter within
old friends   new meetings
amberlit ambience
of the lakeside hotel
plunging and lazing
in the earth-heated water
safe as unborn things
in the amniotic pool.

Without, the winter
prowls like a stalker
through abandoned houses
along wide empty streets
totem poles shiver
in the long wind of history
lonely in his hill cave
the last sasquatch sleeps.

The Defector

I shall have no more affairs
with ghosts in crumbling cottages
to the echo of voiceless laughter
the conversations of chairs
watched from inhabited mirrors
by shadows that cannot rest
before the emberless hearthstones
on rugs of muttering dust.

I shall whisper no more endearments
to earless listening skulls
beside the gravestoned gardens
where fingers grope from the soil
when the moon gapes mad from the sky
on midnights of gelid flame
striking the pits alive,
the lurkers locked in the clay.

I shall bid farewell to my phantoms
my consorts of empty rooms
kiss no more the spectral lips
nor stroke the bodiless limbs.
From these hills of other-than-life
I shall venture the crooked road
to the smug and unsuspecting towns
haunted by flesh and blood.

In the Churchyard

Be still, love, the ghost moves in me again—
the whatever,
the itch without a name.
It has woken like a fox
in the numb passages
to make me make music in the ashen time.

Am I simply mad or was it
more than the earth's outbreathing
rose from the churchyard grass
to claim me when I was seven
till I swayed dazed
by the Norman church six centuries ancient,
where bas-relief faces haunt the walls
and the pews are polished glossy
by a lineage of dutiful buttocks,
reeled among gravestones
locked like mossy grey teeth
to the forefathered ground?

Am I simply mad or was I
truly invaded or taken
by something sudden as a wind
when the sky grew more blue and lucid
than England normally allows
a calligraphy of strange birds
scribbling from the trees
gold on the pious scrolled gates
as I giddied through them
and something forever gone different?

Be still, love, the ghost moves in me again—
the whatever,
the itch without a name.
It has woken like a fox
in the numb passageways
to make me make music in the ashen time.

On Uncharted Seas

There is no orderly way
out of this mortal riddle—
we are seldom packed and ready
on that last decisive day.

Trailing loose ends
we are pulled willy-nilly from the game
full of unspoken last words,
leaving the useless grief of friends.

Into light's last arabesque
we dance dully—
there are clean socks in the drawer,
a final letter lies forever unfinished
on the cold desk.

The blunt facts are these—
death is a mischievous boy
waiting to cut our towropes
to set the boats of us adrift
on uncharted seas.

A Voice from the Edge

for Pat Lowther

I will never forget your voice
on that last day of your days
it ghosted over the phone like audible darkness
strained   sapped   utterly empty
bled of all hope   all joy
the merest echo of you
the voice of someone who faced
the naked unfaceable.

All the unwritten poems
lay stillborn in your brain
never to escape from you
like bright birds
never to slide again from your fingertips
full of wisdom   laughter   pain
never to scratch wonder
from the white waste of a page.

The sea   the woods   the mountains
you loved and celebrated
lay forever beyond your window now
your eyes would not kiss them again
you would become your children's sorrow
in the dark stain of your going
you would become your photographs
the small unfinished legacy of your verse.

But I didn't know   didn't know
I thought I had somehow offended you
I turned the thing to myself
as I too often did then.
And I didn't know   didn't know
that yours was a voice from the edge
that a man corrupted by jealousy
stood at the door of your life
with his hand on the hammer.

The Ravens

Wherever it begins
on whatever cloudsoaked hill
torn by the whip of a tough man's sneer—
humiliated—
gestating poems and poison
crying tears they can't see
I'm still a rigging slave slandering God
wanting to quit when the wind spits water.

They circle strange in the curdled sky
black messengers
bearing indecipherable messages.
Oldtime loggers
named them soulbearers
where you go when you die
to wake feathered and swooping
your fat brain reduced
to a walnut of useful instinct
black wings slicing
through a universe of air—
better than fools bent and cursing
on blasphemous hills.
Bugs burrow   snakes crawl   ravens swoop.

Cold on unknown mountains
I crack my barriers slowly.
Time is only
amorphous mortar
holding the bricks apart.
The cable I hold in my hand
was fashioned by slaves in other factories.
This factory has no roof;
its walls are the world.

I dream of death and ravens,
sky and silence.
The last log takes me,
my arms become feathered,
I flap upward from blood.
Ravens swoop   I swoop with them.

Upwind from Yesterday

Times that burned with pain and beauty
a chaos of friendships and disasters
moments that collapsed like imploded buildings
chances that flickered by and passed
the bitter sound of lost laughter.

Upwind from yesterday
the shape of things alters and twists,
the hurts diminish,
the misapprehensions pack their bags.
We are left with the trembling gist.

A thousand foolish experiences
have scarred me, left me little wiser.
I am a bemused atavist
in a present I barely understand
banging an obsolete typewriter.

These are my passage-rites, my poems
I pass them to you come what may
I offer no apologies, no excuses.
They are only residual echoes I have sifted
upwind from yesterday.

Ghostcamp

A lot of loggers hide dead in these hills
setting chokers eternally
on healed slopes above brush-choked landings
where rusting steampots
crouch sphinxlike and voiceless
and corroded snake cables
twist paralyzed among the ferns
with motion, a steel memory.

In the empty camp that lies
half-ransacked at the northern mouth
of this ransacked valley,
we stand thoughtful among ruin
ancient bull-blocks
sleep like giant turtles in the weeds
heavy two-man powersaws
lie forever unmended in sheds.

Garages full of obsolete bearings
abandoned anvils
blacksmiths and mechanics gone
to whatever random destiny.
The gutted bunkhouse guards echoes
fled dreams of drifted men
with few dreams. The cookshack
guthammer hasn't clanged for years.

I have come full circle—
across the inlet lies Misery Creek
where my brother and I watched camp
one fireseason summer two decades back.
The dead camp sprawls around us.
I can't speak. It's too strange.
Log long enough, you're bound to stumble
across your own bootprints in the end.

Books by Peter Trower

Poetry
Moving Through the Mystery (1969)
Between the Sky and the Splinters (1974)
The Alders and Others (1976)
Ragged Horizons (1978)
Bush Poems (1978)
Goosequill Snags (1982)
The Slidingback Hills (1986)
Unmarked Doorways (1989)
Hitting the Bricks (1997)
Chainsaws in the Cathedral (1999)
A Ship Called Destiny (2000)
There Are Many Ways (2002)

Prose: *Rough and Ready Times* (non-fiction, 1993), *Grogan's Cafe* (novel, 1993), *Dead Man's Ticket* (novel, 1996), *The Judas Hills* (novel, 2000)

CD's: *Sidewalks and Sidehills* (2003), *Kisses in the Whiskey* (2004)

Websites: www.petertrower.com, www.harbourpublishing.com/petertrower

Title Index

First Appeared